Not Far From The Tree

Eric Otis Simmons

The people and events in "Not Far From The Tree," are based on my life experiences and are intended only to tell my story.

Dedication

In Loving Memory of Jean Wiletta Simmons

To my Mother, who was the sweetest, brightest and most caring person I've ever known. God put my Mom, one of his Angels, on this earth to care for, love, and nurture others. None benefited more from her love than I, who was touched daily by her bright light. I am comforted in the knowledge she is with God and in a place where she always wanted to be, and he is saying to her, "Servant of Mine, Well Done!"

And

To young black men and women who like me were/are raised by a single Mom. Keep your head up, eyes to the sky, believe in yourself, and to hell with people like George Karl who suggest not having a black Father around is a detriment!

Acknowledgements

To my beautiful wife, Cynthia. Thank you for being by my side these past 37 years. Without question, aside from my Mom, you are the most genuine person I've ever met. There's nothing fake or pretentious about you. I love and admire you for being "wired" that way. Thank you for being a great mother, a devoted Christian, and for being level headed and a calming influence for the kids and me. If more people on this earth walked life's path the way you do, the world would be a better place.

To my young adults, Derek, Dominique, and Kevin. Thank you for being obedient children (#Most of The Time) and for striving and dreaming of doing great things with your lives.

To those Relatives, Coaches, Teachers, Friends and Business Leaders who inspired and motivated me through example. Thanks for showing me, "What Good Looks Like."

Preface

When I started writing my Memoir, my aim was to provide a "Leave Behind," so to speak, for my young adults about their family history and reveal more about myself and my life's work to them. God moves in mysterious ways, though. Just when I thought I had told my children "My Story," I realized I had missed the mark. At the root of "My Story" is the motivation and determination embedded in me, a black man, by my black Mother – who raised me as a single Mom. It was through her and God; I managed to defy academic, athletic, business and social myths/stereotypes. Any success I've had in life, large or small, is primarily attributable to the infusion of "can do" instilled in me by my Mother. She is at the very core of "My Story."

My goals for this Memoir are 1). Provide my young adults with information about their Family Tree and their Old Man. 2). Share "My Story" to inspire others, particularly young Black men and women raised by a single Mom. My hope is I give others the courage to try and do the unthinkable and not be afraid to come out of their comfort zone. I hope you will be bold enough to knock down walls and try new things in life, like I, such as writing a Memoir to tell your story.

Cognizant other black men have told "their story," each of ours is unique, in its own way. Enclosed is my inimitable story.

Forward

by Kevin Simmons

I have had the honor to be alongside Eric Simmons in many aspects of my life. These include struggles, temptations, excitement, and many other facets of existence a person may go through. Specifically, an African American male in a society that still struggles with racism. This man's story can be applied to many in the Black community, particularly male and female athletes that have grown up with one parent or no parent. This book isn't just a glimpse into the past of a family's history; it entails stories that provide the reader with hope and motivation for their life. "Not Far From The Tree" is also a spotlight into the experiences of an African American male and how he and other blacks lived during the 60's and 70's when racial tensions were high.

My father is someone that I look up to as a respected man of character, integrity, and humility. He takes pride in his various crafts, and it has translated into being an example for his family, friends, and people around him. When I think about the credibility of Eric Simmons, a timeline of his accolades and successes come to mind. From his "heart over height" mentality to make Auburn's basketball team, against all the odds, to obtaining various leadership positions while working at IBM and other Fortune 500 companies, he has the hardware to prove he knows what he is talking about. The key thing about Eric Simmons is that he has always been humble throughout his life. While reading the book, I hope you will be able to see how a small African American male from Little Rock, Arkansas made a name for himself.

Readers will find historical information about the Simmons' family and understand the origins of where Eric Simmons has come from. I'm hopeful that in reading this book, people will further understand how important family lineage is and more importantly, pick up on key life lessons throughout its contents. Life is a never-ending battle with few ups and many downs. The times we live in now, are such, people have numerous resources to help them overcome trials and tribulations. I believe this book is going to help individuals, raised by a single parent, or no parent, that are going through or have gone through similar circumstances as my Dad. This book is a guide for people who can relate to Eric Simmons and find themselves looking for hope and encouragement. "Not Far From The Tree" is a great read, and at the end of the book, I believe readers will see that they too are not far from the tree.

Introduction

I'm Eric Otis Simmons, and I am a Challenge Acceptor (#CA). I love proving people wrong. Tell me I can't do something, and more times than not, I'll do it! Need a few bits of proof? A Senior Executive with an Asia-Pacific company once told me he didn't feel comfortable doing business with an American company. Six months later, he procured $25 million worth of business from me. People told me I was too small to walk on and make Auburn University's basketball team. At 5' 7" and 147 pounds, I made the team. A guy once told me I'd never work for the likes of IBM, AT&T or GE. Well, I worked in Sales and Sales Management for all three. Someone said to me, "Oh, you'll never marry that girl." Well, I married "that girl," and we've been together for 37 years. I've been personally thanked by Governor George Corley Wallace for a job well done in selling his office an IBM computer system. He was the same man that stood at "The Door" of the University of Alabama to fight entry of blacks into the school. I was the only black man in the room when I closed sales of $500,000 and up in Brussels, Paris, and Hong Kong. When I was told I'd never learn to water ski on my first time out, I did and jokingly proclaimed myself, "The First Black Man on Skis."

How does a black man, raised by a single Mom, do all of this when "society" says it can't happen? Well, it did happen, because my Mom instilled in me, "seeds" of knowledge, which were - I could do anything and be anything I wanted - if I just put my mind to it. I believed what my Mom told me, and I refused to let her down.

Contents

Chapter 1

A Child is Born

It was May 18, 1956, around 11:00 P.M. Otis Davis Simmons paced the halls of University Hospital nervously awaiting news of his wife's (Jean Wiletta) and child's status. He couldn't imagine what could be taking so long. As time passed by, Otis grew more, and more anxious, and began fearing the worst. He and Jean, or "Willy," as he affectionately called her, arrived at Little Rock's University Hospital around 8:45 that night. She had been prepped and taken to the delivery room around 9:30. Weary of his pacing, Nannie Belle, Otis' Mother, who had arrived by train a week earlier from Kansas City to assist the young couple, said, "Otis, why don't you go outside and smoke your pipe to relax? I'll come get you when the nurse comes." Otis replied, "I'm out of tobacco. I've smoked the entire pouch since we've been here."

Inside the delivery room, Dr. Eva Dodge had worries of her own. Jean and Otis' baby had, at some point near the end of the pregnancy, flipped and the buttocks were appearing first. Dr. Dodge worked feverishly to try and turn the baby so that it would be born headfirst. The baby was having none of it, however. Eventually, Dr. Dodge managed to turn the baby so she could grab its feet. At 12:26 A.M. on May 19th, Otis and Jean had a son. They named him Eric Otis Simmons.

1

There was joy all around the little house on 1110 Izard Street. The parents were aglow about their new son, and Nannie Belle was every bit as proud. Friends, faculty, and students from Philander Smith College, where the couple worked, streamed through the house to see the new baby boy. Jean, who was a Graduate Student Instructor at the College, had received a wager from her students whereby if the child were a boy, she would have to nickname him Butch. Jean playfully took up her students on the name bet. Much to their delight, she and Otis honored their wager by nicknaming the newborn boy, Butch.

Otis, Nannie Belle, and Jean looking over Butch

Although somewhat embellished, these were actual events surrounding my birth.

Chapter 2

In a League, All Their Own

I wasn't born to just any two parents. Years ago, my parents and I were sitting at the kitchen table when I said, "Both of you have told me you used to recite Shakespeare to one another in bed. I've never heard you quote Shakespeare before." Dad looked at Mom and said, "Why don't we do our favorite piece?" The next thing I knew, they were going back and forth alternating between verses of Shakespeare with a gleam in their eyes. I said, "Wait a minute guys. It was that look that probably brought me into this world!" They erupted into laughter. Dad nearly fell on the floor howling, and Mom was in tears. When they composed themselves, I followed with, "I have to ask you guys something serious. Something very serious." They looked at me with concern on their faces and in near unison replied, "Sure son. You can ask us anything." I inquired, "Am I adopted?" Then there was more howling, table pounding, and laughter between them. They assured me I wasn't adopted.

Mom and Dad met in 1953 at Philander Smith College where he was the new Choir Director and Voice Instructor. She was a recent Pre-Law graduate and Assistant to the College's President, Dr. Lafayette Harris.

Dad and Mom during their Philander Smith days

After graduating from Sumner High School, Dad served four years in the Army where he rose to the rank of Second Lieutenant before being Honorably Discharged. He received his Bachelor (1953), Master (1958), and Ph.D. (1965) in Music Education from the University of Kansas. Dad also spoke German and French. From 1948-1949, he attended the Kansas City Conservatory of Music to study voice with Endre Kreachmann, formally the leading baritone of the Paris Opera Company. He was the only African-American to sing in the select male chorus of the Conservatory during a presentation of the "Alto Rhapsody" by Brahms with Blanche Thebom of the Metropolitan Opera as soloist. Dad also sang as a soloist with the Kansas City Symphony band.

When she was in the fourth grade, Mom had to drop out of school for the year due to an illness. When she returned the next year, Mom performed so well, she skipped two grade levels (fourth, and fifth grades). After graduating from high school, my Mother received numerous scholarship offers to attend college. She chose Philander Smith College, a Methodist school in Little Rock, Arkansas upon receipt of a full four-year scholarship from the United Methodist Church. In 1953, after only three years of attendance, Mom graduated with a Bachelor of Arts degree in Pre-Law, with Honors, from Philander Smith. Shortly afterward, she was accepted to attend Boston University's School of Law and The University of Arkansas' College of Education Master's Degree program. She decided to go to the University of Arkansas.

Mom and Dad married May 17, 1954. He was 30; she was 22. Their wedding was held at the President's House on the campus of Philander Smith College.

The newlyweds

On January 28, 1956, roughly five months before I was born, Mom became one of the first, if not the first, African-American women to receive a Master of Education degree from the University of Arkansas. Following, she received the prestigious Ford Foundation Fellow award to begin her study towards a PH.D. in Education at the University. To better understand the significance of the award, in 2016, only 60 Ford Foundation Fellow awards were bestowed nationally. Mom's PH.D. research was a part of the "Arkansas Experiment in Teacher Education" which was a new and controversial program combining internship and professional study. Apparently, with me needing so much of her attention as a toddler, Mom ultimately decided to cease pursuit of her Doctorate.

On September 15, 1959, after nearly five years of marriage, my parents divorced. I was three years old at the time. My parents never told me why they divorced. I have my guesses, though. My thinking is, in the 1950's, women were expected to be subservient to men and know that their place was "in the home." Mom was the antithesis of such thinking. Dad was a highly driven, articulate, intelligent black man with a higher IQ than most white males he encountered. Mom was every bit of Dad's match intellectually. Add to the mix; she was a black woman. Without question, both my parents were far ahead of the times in which they lived. Of the two, Dad's ego and tremendous pride were far greater than Mom's. When I add it up, I find it inconceivable the two could have coexisted together, under one roof, for an extended period, especially in that particular era. Put another way; I have concluded, *"**My parents were like poles, and they ended up repelling one another.**"*

Chapter 3

Otis Alexander Bailey

A sociologist once wrote, "We live in an unpredictable world *full of surprises*, good, and bad." Truer words perhaps have never been spoken. A little bit over a year after my Dad passed away, I decided to either keep or get rid of some of his belongings I had been reluctant to let go of. In a two-drawer mahogany file cabinet of his, I noticed a folder entitled, "Birth Certificates/Name Change." "How could I have missed this folder previously?" I thought. Inside, there was a certificate of birth.

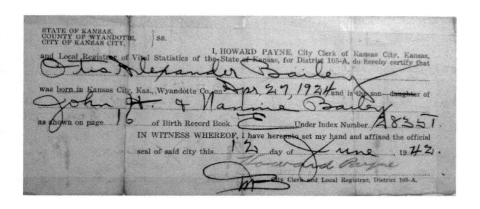

I wondered why Dad would have this and if this person was him. The birth date and Mother's first name matched his and my Grandmother. "Who was John H. Bailey?" I wondered. I was confused and needed some answers quickly! An immediate one was in another document inside the folder of which there were two copies. It was a court document with the heading, "… **IN THE MATTER OF THE APPLICATION OF OTIS ALEXANDER BAILEY TO CHANGE HIS NAME TO OTIS DAVIS SIMMONS.**" I was floored! On March 31, 1948, a Judge granted the petition for a name change. The permission had occurred about a month before Dad turned 24-years-old. **Talk about a major surprise here!**

I knew Jesse Simmons was Dad's Stepfather but didn't know Dad was born Otis Alexander Bailey, and his biological father was John H. Bailey. I wondered if my Mom ever knew this. I still could not figure out why Dad changed his middle name to Davis though. I began wondering, "What other surprises might be in store for me as relates to my family?" I needed some answers, but unfortunately, the relatives who could have possibly given them to me had all passed away. To get answers to my questions, I realized I needed to do some genealogical research.

Chapter 4

My Ancestry Hunt

In many black families, historical information is passed on by word of mouth and unfortunately tends to wither away over time – especially when relatives become deceased. Cognizant of such, I am making "The Simmons Family Tree" available to my children and family members online so they can expand on it going forward. I encourage and challenge them to find out information about the slave ships our ancestors came over on, who our slave masters were and to one day visit our homeland.

One day, late winter of 2013, I was at a business lunch meeting with my company President and several other Managers. The President shared how he pulled together his family tree using an online service named, "Ancestry.com" or "Ancestry" for short. He showed us a picture of his family shield which he had discovered using the service and spoke with immense pride about his Italian heritage. He asked me where I was from and I told him Little Rock, Arkansas. When I got home, I was embarrassed to tears. I was 57 years old, and I didn't know where I was from. Sure, I was born in Little Rock, Arkansas, but I am **actually from Africa**, and sadly, I didn't even know what part. I made up my mind, the next time someone asked me where I was from, I would know exactly where! On April 9th of that same year, I ordered a subscription to "Ancestry" and later began building my family tree. I started with my Mother's side first because I had more information than on my Dad's side, which was very limited.

To find out about my African roots, I ordered two DNA saliva test kits from "Ancestry." I used the first one to capture my youngest son's (Kevin) saliva, and the second mine. My intent with Kevin's test was to obtain information on my wife's genealogy. When both test results were made available online for review, I studied the results thoroughly.

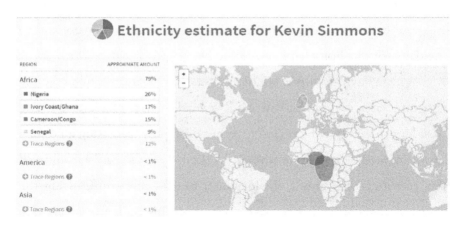

DNA results for Kevin Simmons

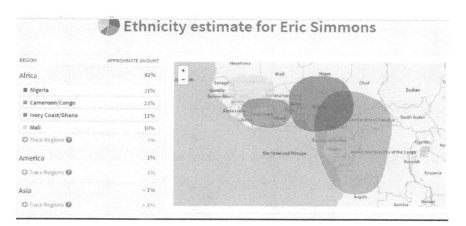

DNA results for Eric Simmons

At last, I had the answer to the question of where I was from. Now, I could with confidence, pride, and dignity say, "**I am from West Africa and am predominately Nigerian!**" No more tears again about me not knowing.

Kevin's test results yielded 132 Ancestry subscribers with whom he shared DNA traces. The list of people ranged from being likely second to eighth cousins. My list contained 139 users who ranged from being likely first to eighth cousins. With this information in hand, I decided to send a message to those that allowed other Ancestry members their contact info, to make them aware of Kevin's and my DNA results. I focused on individuals who had already built large family trees in the "service" and who were rated as "Extremely High" or "High" regarding the likelihood of being a first to the fourth cousin. Ten of the 18 members (61%) I contacted responded back. Of these, two quickly notified me as to our relationship.

With Mom's side of the family tree underway, I sought to obtain Dad's original birth certificate. I felt it would possibly have more information about my biological Grandfather John H. Bailey. On June 29, 2016, I contacted the Kansas Department of Health, and Environment (KDHE) to order an original copy of Dad's birth certificate. A Department employee referred me to the online forms I needed to complete to receive a copy of the document. Three weeks passed, and I had not heard back from KDHE. I called and learned the researcher assigned to me had become confused about Dad's two names and had stopped his investigation. In speaking with the investigator, I realized I had failed to send the court petition which granted Dad's name change. With the matter cleared up, about a week later I received Dad's original birth certificate. I was ecstatic! Now, I had what I needed to begin putting together pieces of the puzzle as relates to his side of the family.

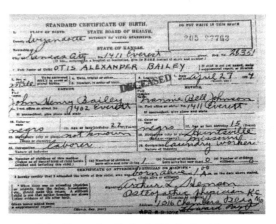

Otis Alexander Bailey's Birth Certificate

I spent countless hours researching my patriarchal side. From starting with only ten known patrilineal family members, I have found about 100 relatives dating all the way back to 1799. These are all either related to my Grandmother (Nannie Belle) or my StepGrandfather (Jesse Simmons). My investigation of John H. Bailey revealed his middle name was Henry. I have researched thousands of people named John Bailey, or similar, and have not been able to find out more about him other than the information on the birth certificate. Also, I have not been able to find a marriage license for him and my Grandmother. Not having my biological Grandfather's place of birth written on Dad's birth certificate has significantly thwarted my investigative efforts.

On June 15, 1926, Grandmother married Andy A. Davis. He was 27, and she was 18. As of this writing, I have not been able to find any other information about him. I did find something interesting in the 1930 United States Census, however. Dad was living with my Great Grandfather (Merritt Johnson) and Great Grandmother (Fannie Bagby Johnson). His full name is shown as Otis Davis. I've concluded the surname Davis must be the reason behind Dad's middle name change. When the 1940 U.S. Census was taken, Grandma was listed as the spouse of Jesse Simmons. They lived in Detroit, Michigan with their two children Otis Simmons (age 15) and my Aunt Norma Jean Simmons (age 14). I have been unable to find out when Grandmother and Jesse were married. In the Court document, Dad states he was requesting a name change to avoid confusion when seeking

13

employment. This would make sense to me, particularly if someone requested his birth certificate.

Mom was born September 3, 1931, in Eufaula, Alabama to William Dewitt Moore and Flossie Mae Moore. He was 24, and she was 19. I learned during my research that Flossie's maiden name was also Moore. The two were unrelated. Strangely, on my Mother's side, there was another occurrence of married relatives with the same last name who were unrelated. In this case, a Brown married a Brown. Like Dad's, my Mother's birth certificate turned out to be quite a surprise - although less shocking. The Alabama Department of Health's Bureau of Vital Statistics incorrectly listed her as being born a boy named Clennie Mae Moore. About one month after Mom was born, the Department corrected the name to read Wiletta Victora Moore. Mom was named after her Aunt and Grandmother. To this day, I have no idea how Mom came to be called Jean Wiletta.

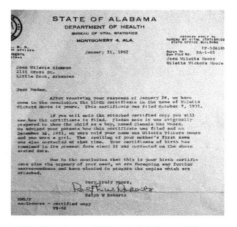

Clarification of Mom's birth certificate

Granddad William was one of five children born to my Great Grandparents John William Moore and Victoria McCullough. Granddad's siblings were: Cortelyou Joseph, John Purifoy, Crawford, and Wiletta. My Great Grandparents apparently felt it important their children pass down names through the family – a notion which I find quite noble. To date, there have been two generations of Victoria or similar, two generations of Wiletta, three generations of John or similar, and three generations of Cortelyou Joseph within the Moore family.

Per her death certificate, my Grandmother Flossie Mae died when Mom was nine years old. So, I wondered, how then and why did Mom end up in Akron, Ohio being raised by Eula Mae Nevels whom I grew up knowing as my Grandmother? No one had ever said or told me otherwise. Where was Granddad William during this time? Once again, I found myself needing answers.

Mom at a young age

My "Ancestry" research revealed Flossie Mae was the only child of Cleveland Moore and Mary Brown, my Great Grandparents. Mary was one of 8 children born to James and Lizzie Brown. One of Mary's siblings was her sister Eula Lee. Somehow, apparently, Eula Lee became being called Eula Mae. Perhaps her full name was Eula Mae Lee Brown. On an insurance policy, I found after Mom passed away, it shows Eula as her Aunt. In a 1962 Department of Defense Personnel Security Questionnaire that Mom signed, Eula is listed as her Legal Guardian. In the same document, Mom is shown as living in Akron in 1937 which would have made her six years old. In Eula's obituary, Mom is listed as her adopted daughter. Confused by all of this, I called my cousin Barbara Brown to share my discovery. Barbara confirmed Eula was my Great Aunt. I also learned Barbara was Eula's Granddaughter – a fact I never knew. I was 59 years old when I learned all of this. Life is full of surprises indeed.

I still didn't have the answer as to how and why Mom ended up in Akron, Ohio with my "Grandmother" Eula. Granddad William and Grandmother Flossie Mae were still alive in 1937. I have learned when doing genealogical research, and you come across unanswered questions or a dead end, you should avail yourself of all known resources (if there are any) or make logical conclusions/assumptions as to what may have happened. I ended up calling Barbara (who was born and raised in Akron) again. Apparently, before my Mom turned 6, Grandmother Flossie Mae became terminally ill and was unable to care for Mom to the extent she would have liked. As I listened to

Barbara, I do recall hearing such from my Mother when I was young. Grandmother Flossie died in 1940. Apparently, she and Granddad William were desirous of a female raising my Mother and realized the strain it would have been on Granddad raising Mom alone as a single parent. As best as I could figure out, there were two potential female options for my maternal Grandparents to reach out to at the time. One was Mom's Aunt Wiletta who was single and age 24. The other was Eula who was married and age 30-31. I don't doubt Grandma and Granddad felt Eula offered more maturity, age wise, and stability, marriage wise, to raise Mom.

After not knowing a lot about my family tree and history, to date, I have identified about 700 family members and counting. I fully expect to find other new and surprising twists along the way. I am excited to leave this information behind for my children and their children's children.

Chapter 5

Otis Davis Simmons

My Dad was the quintessential Renaissance man. He was an artist, composer, opera singer, immaculate dresser, multilingual, author, former athlete and much, much, more. How a black man could do the things he did, at the levels he did, and in the eras in which he did, is incomprehensible to me. My father was living proof a black man could be immensely successful in America. I looked up to him and admired him because he had blazed a trail of success that I not only wanted to emulate and follow but sought to exceed.

My adulation for Dad, along with its peaks, did have its valleys, though. There were times, growing up when I felt his career and the "finer things in life" were more important to him than his wife and child. This emotion would leave me feeling angry and frustrated with him. I would also blame Dad for his and Mom's divorce. Why didn't he write, call, or travel to see me, I wondered. I viewed him as being an egotistical and self-centered human being. Perhaps my feelings and thoughts were like other young black men and women whom grow up without a father and are raised by a single Mom. I always found it interesting, whenever I would express my feelings to Mom about Dad, she would never say a bad thing about him. I mean never. Was this due to her innate kindness, and or her biblical belief around not judging others for so shall you be judged? Mom always spoke glowingly to me about my father. His accomplishments were so remarkable; it seemed as if someone had made it all up. I was 13 years old when I finally got to meet Dr. Otis Davis Simmons. Quite naturally, I had mixed emotions. On the one hand, I was very excited. On the other, I was mad at him for not being in my life. It turned out he was everything my mother had told me about him. He was about 5 foot 11, dark skinned and had an athletic build. There was an air about him.

Perhaps, unlike many black men and women who have walked in my shoes, my story turned out to have a happy ending with my Dad. When I reached adulthood, he and I would sit down and chat for hours on end. I guess each of us was trying to make up for lost time. I could see it in his eyes, his recognition of how much he had missed not being around to help raise me. To his credit, he tried very hard to bridge the gap between father and son. Boy, we had some enjoyable times together. We would laugh until we cried about his and my life experiences. Sometimes, I would throw in a risqué joke that would leave him hollering. I'd have a beer in hand, and most times he would have his favorite drink, Chivas Regal in a crystal glass. His Chivas always had to be in a crystal whiskey glass, and of course, he would smoke his omnipresent pipe which was his "trademark."

Photograph   Dad's Self Portrait

Dad was born and raised in Kansas City, Kansas. He
graduated from Northeast Junior High School and then went on to
attend Sumner High. At Sumner, Dad was a straight "A" student, Class
Historian, winner of a four-state art contest and excelled in football
and track and field. In football, he was a wide receiver for the Spartans.
In track, Pops ran the half mile (i.e. 880-yard dash). He used to tell me
one story repeatedly that would always leave me in stitches. Sumner
had a game against an all-black team from Oklahoma who stepped off
its bus wearing no uniforms. Spartans players laughed hysterically
about what they were seeing. Apparently, the other school couldn't
afford uniforms for its players, so Sumner loaned the team its practice
uniforms.

Upon seeing a cute Sumner cheerleader he liked, Dad made up
his mind he was going to "show out" in the game to impress her.
During the contest, Sumner's quarterback called a play in which my
father was to run a "post pattern." The quarterback threw the ball
high, so Dad had to jump up to catch it. The next thing he

remembered was being in the locker room. Thinking it was halftime, he told his Coach he was ready to get back in the game. His Coach replied, "Hell, Otis, the game is over! You got knocked out, and we lost!" Each time, after telling the story, Dad would say to me in his basso profondo voice, "Son, I learned a valuable lesson that day. It was, to never underestimate your opponent! I mean, never, never, ever underestimate your opponent! Do you understand me, son?" Dad was great at telling a story but was probably better at imparting knowledge and wisdom. Whenever he would tell the story, he was giving me a "seed" of knowledge and wisdom.

Another one of my favorite stories Dad would tell was when he competed in the high school version of the Kansas Relays, arguably the most prestigious track and field event in the country for high school and college athletes. Today, athletes from all over the U.S. take part in the Kansas Relays which is now an Olympic team track and field pre-qualifying event. The meet Dad participated in consisted of athletes from the Midwest. Leading up to the event, my old man's Track Coach came up to him, and said, "Otis, we need to talk. The fastest man in the 880-yard dash in the Midwest will be competing at the Kansas Relays. Thus, we've got to change our strategy as to how you run the race." The Coach went on to say, "Rather than stay in the back of the pack like you normally do, I want you to take off like a bat out of hell, get in front, stay there, and don't you dare look back! Got it?" Dad thought his Coach was nuts. He preferred running from behind so he could size up his opponents. Heretofore, Dad's stamina,

21

and "kick" over the last 200 yards made him virtually unbeatable. Now he was being asked to run in a manner which was completely out of his "comfort zone."

On the day of the race, Pops executed what his Coach had told him. He went out fast, took the lead, and kept it. With about 200 yards to go, Dad listened for the "fastest" runner's footsteps on the cinder track. He never heard a sound. He ended up winning the race resoundingly. The "seed" for me here was, "Son, don't be afraid to get out of your comfort zone. Get out front, take the lead, and never look back."

Following his graduation from high school, Dad joined the Army. His first tour of duty was in Hersfeld, Germany in 1945. Ultimately, he was promoted to Tech Sergeant. On his next tour of duty in the Philippines, at the age of 21, Captain Eddie J. Lee recommended Dad for promotion to the rank of Second Lieutenant. On November 18, 1946, Captain Lee wrote a glowing recommendation about Pop and his efficiency, versatility, leadership and organizational skills. Ensuing, Dad went on to pass the Officer Candidate test and was promoted to Second Lieutenant on February 17, 1947, in Manila. He would go on to be awarded the Good Conduct Medal and was Honorably Discharged in 1948.

During our conversations, it was evident to me how proud Dad was of being a graduate of the University of Kansas. Career wise, he felt his highlight was when he became the first Dean of the School of Music at Alabama State University (ASU). There, his vision was to gain National Accreditation for the Music Department and to have a "State-of-the-Art" music building constructed.   Through his leadership, both came to fruition.   After he had retired, Dad received ASU's "Legacy Award in Music Education."

Dr. Otis Davis Simmons with his Doctoral Dissertation: "Neurophysiology, and Muscular Function of the Vocal Mechanism: Implications for Singers, and Teachers of Singing."

A few years after into his retirement, it didn't surprise me when Dad called, at the age of seventy-six, to inform me he was coming out of retirement and going back to work as an Adjunct Professor of Music at Troy University Montgomery. He stayed at Troy, where he taught music classes, for fourteen years until his passing. The "seed" for me here was, "Son, continue passing your baton of knowledge on to others so they too may prosper and cross the finish line victorious!" In an Alabama State University article entitled, "**ASU Family Mourns Loss of Legendary Music Dean,**" Dad was lauded for being a consummate perfectionist and an important part of the history of the Music Department at ASU."

Dad's mantra was, "**Cogito Ergo Sum**." He roared like a lion every time he said it. When I was 19, he asked me to interpret it. I said, "Dad, I'm not taking Latin in college." He replied, "Go ahead. Give it a try." I responded with, "Cogito means cognition or think. Ergo sounds like erstwhile, and Sum is a derivation of summation. Cogito Ergo Sum denotes: Think, therefore the sum. As a man thinketh so is he. I am the sum of my thoughts. If I believe it, I can achieve it." I asked, "How did I do?" Dad took a sip of Chivas Regal, and then a long puff on his pipe. He blew out a large billow of smoke, and said, "Son. Now you're thinking like a scholar!"

Chapter 6

Jean Wiletta Simmons

My Mother was like a "Rainbow from Heaven" - replete in all her splendor. There was just something about her. She had this radiant glow. My youngest son, Kevin, had this to say about his grandmother, "Grammy was hard working and one of the most influential women I've had in my life. She would continuously show her love and affection for my siblings and me through her actions. She always put our needs before her own and went the extra mile to make sure we were comfortable. Her character made me want to be a better person. Grammy's kindness was prevalent in all aspects of her life. Her nurture and love for others made Wiletta Simmons the definition of servitude. This Christ-like manner made others want to emulate her every day. Although she was kind, she also would not be taken advantage of. Her resilience and fighting nature made her one of the many women to change history, and do things unthinkable for a woman, a matter of fact an African American. If you knew my Grandmother, you would be proud to be in the same room with her.

But if you were related to her...you were honored to see how God blessed this woman of courage."

In a 2005 "Commentary" article for US Black Engineer & IT magazine entitled, "MS. SIMMONS' CHILDREN," Sylvester Foley III provided his thoughts on having met my Mother for the first time. Following is an excerpt from the article,

US Black Engineer & IT Mar-Apr 2005

MS. SIMMONS' CHILDREN
By Sylvester Foley III

"I attended a dinner at Tuskegee University not long ago…

Entering the room, I stood behind a quiet, elegant lady being surrounded, and hugged by these energetic students. As I introduced myself, she said that her name was Ms. Wiletta Simmons. I held her chair as she sat down, and as that table was nearly full, I started to find an open seat at a nearby table. But Simmons took my hand, and told

me to sit next to her, smiling as she said, "You are one of my children."
When I offered that I was not a graduate of Tuskegee, she again took
my hand and drew me closer to her. She quietly said, "You are now
one of my children, and a part of this family gathered here."

Ms. Simmons has been the executive assistant, scheduling
coordinator, problem solver, and personal mentor of engineering
deans at Tuskegee University for longer than most of the students
gathered that evening have been alive. With her characteristic poise,
grace, and boundless love, she has nurtured and guided countless
faculty, students, and alumni. Ms. Simmons has touched innumerable
lives, and by her quiet example of service to others has personally
inspired thousands of people with whom she has come in contact.
Every one of these individuals was claimed by Ms. Simmons without
any questions about their background, education, or political
ideology."

Kevin's and Foley's view sum up my Mom in a nutshell.
Jean Wiletta Simmons stood 5 feet tall and weighed, as she would say,
"100 pounds soaking wet." Mom had a brisk walk that would leave
people trying to keep up with her gasping for air. You would have
thought she was headed to put out a fire or something. Truth be told,
Mom knew she had God's work to do, and there was no time for
"fiddling around" as she used to say. When she met you for the first
time, there was always a warm handshake and an engaging smile. Once
Mom got to know you, my Mother greeted you with a hug. My wife,
kids, and I called it her "Bear Hug" because you literally couldn't

27

breathe when she hugged you. She was pouring all her heart and soul into the recipient with the embrace. You could feel the love coming through, and you knew it was genuine.

My Mother and I had a 52-year relationship together. As a single Mom, she implanted in me "seeds of knowledge" around how to memorize things, how to prepare for public speaking engagements, enunciation, the importance of being on time, strategic planning, how to treat people and a whole lot more. We didn't have much when I was growing up, but I never knew it. To me, it seemed like we had a lot. I guess Mom just had a way of "filling up" my life like that. I owe all of my good qualities to her. My bad ones are completely on me. During my time with her, I never heard Mom say a negative word about another human being. Willy, Jean, Wiletta, or Tootsie as Grandmother Eula affectionately called her, was the embodiment of a loving, caring and giving person. There was nothing fake or pretentious about her or the love she had for others. Mom was a deeply religious person who knew the Bible front to back. In fact, as I look back at her life, she lived the Bible. She could recite scripture and verse without even thinking about it or having to look it up. By no means was Mom perfect, but then who is. Whenever she would accidentally blurt out a curse word, she would instinctively say, "Whoops, I mean shucks!" Next, she would chuckle so hard at herself; her shoulders would shake.

Mom had a can of "whip ass" in that small body of hers too. I was home for the summer after my sophomore year of college and had been playing basketball every day. She had noticed I hadn't been washing dishes or cleaning up behind myself. My Mother gave me clear instructions before she went to work one day to have the house "Spic and Span" when she got back. Well, I played ball most of the day, came home and didn't clean up the house as told.

I was reading the sports section of the newspaper when Mom arrived. She looked around the kitchen and said, "Butch, didn't I tell you to do something? Didn't I tell you to clean up this house?" I replied, "Yeah Mom, I'll get to it in a minute." My Mother said, "Stand up young man!" I stood up and the next thing I knew, Mom had me up in the air over her shoulders with her fingernails piercing my armpits until they started bleeding. She walked with me, while I was up in the air, and slammed me against the wall. I weighed 157 pounds at the time. While pressed against the wall, I looked down, and my toes couldn't touch the floor. I looked to my left and saw the top of our green wall mounted rotary dial telephone. I remember vividly thinking to myself, "Holy sh$%! I'm going to die!" I was scared out of my mind as Mom gave me an "airborne lecture." Suffice it to say, when she let me down, and to this day, I have never cleaned house so thoroughly. I even scrubbed the toilet with a toothbrush! As for the kitchen, you could have eaten off the floor when I finished. The "seed" she planted was, "Don't make Mom mad. She brought me into this world and Mom sure as hell could take me out of it." Suffice it to say; I was never flippant with my Mother again.

Every morning, Mom would put on a pot of coffee before preparing breakfast. She always had to have her cup of morning coffee to start off her day. I could hear her silver coffee pot percolating a room away, and smell the aroma of Maxwell House, her favorite blend, throughout the house. Scrambled eggs, bacon or sausage, hash browns, grits or oatmeal, French or plain toast, you name it; breakfast was a treat. Mom was a fantastic cook who enjoyed preparing meals for others. People used to say, "Man, Jean knows she can burn." This was the ultimate compliment for a "black" cook.

Mom was a voracious reader. Without fail, she would read the entire newspaper every day – sometimes twice it seems. Her favorite book was the Bible. My Mother also loved solving crossword puzzles, which she did daily. She was so good at unraveling brain teasers that for years, she would only decode them with an ink pen. I estimate Mom solved about 18,980 crossword puzzles (one puzzle a day for 52 years, and got 18,979 of them right. I only saw her get one crossword incorrect and it was a New York Times puzzle. She transposed two letters, and that led to one misspelled word. That was the only crossword I ever saw her miss. That's a 99.99% accuracy rate. Problem-solving was another "seed" she planted in me. To this day, I thoroughly enjoy crossword puzzles but am no match for my Mom.

My Mother's mind was like a steel trap. Her recollection of dates, times, events and what she had read was mind boggling. She also had a clairvoyant-like gift. She would have dreams that would come true. She'd say to me, "Butch, I need to call so and so (with so

30

and so being the person's name). They've been on my mind lately. I had a dream about them. I just can't shake it." Invariably, her dream would be correct. I saw this occur time and time again. Admittedly, this "gift," as I called it, used to freak me out.

Growing up, Mom doted on me. It wasn't "child worship" by any means. When I became a man, sometimes I would feel uncomfortable with her doting. Afterward, I would feel bad because it was just in her nature to love unconditionally. I would have to remind myself I was, perhaps, her reason for living and what kept her alive all those years we were together. It took me a while to understand and fully appreciate this.

Mom and me as a newborn   Me and Mom on my first birthday

After Mom and Dad had divorced, she and I continued to live in Little Rock. She spent nine years working at Philander Smith where she served as Executive Assistant to four of the school's Presidents. In between, Mom worked two years with the Martin Company which at that time was a contractor on a "Classified" project for the United

States Air Force base in Little Rock. Whenever I would ask her what kind of work she was doing, she'd say, "Son, I can't talk about it. It's Classified." At the age of nine, I thought that was so cool. I envisioned my Mom being a spy, working on some secret mission. Years later, after she had passed, I came across some documents and learned her work revolved around the Titan II Missile Project. I remember thinking, "Now how cool was that?"

Mom worked extremely hard to support the two of us. I didn't realize quite how hard until I came across a three-page letter she wrote on November 6, 1969, to Philander Smith's Board of Trustees. In it, she admonished the Board for not having given her a raise in several years. Following is a snippet of points she wrote in the letter. "Since the age of 18, except three years, I have worked at Philander Smith College. Therefore, I am uniquely aware of her problems and her potentials. I have worked since November 5, 1964, without a vacation. I've worked on Saturday's almost constantly even though other office assistants, for the most part, as of June 1, 1968, have not had to work on Saturdays. Also, I have worked through most holidays and recess periods, including the Christian Vacation days. I've also worked on Sundays when necessary and sometimes as much as 23 hours at a time." I have never received or requested any overtime compensation, which when the hours are added up would equal better than a half year's salary."

The underlying tone in the remainder of the letter was, "If you don't give me a raise, which I more than deserve, you can kiss my black a#$ goodbye!" In the 32-years I spent in Corporate America, the entire letter was the best butt kicking, "request for a raise" justification I have ever read! Mom was not subtle in the message. The "seed" for me here was, "Have all of your facts together to validate your position/stance. Once done, it's okay to fire away." Like I said, "My Mom had a can of whip a#$!"

Chapter 7

The Early Years

Growing up, I was a happy, outgoing, inquisitive and talkative child. I talked so much, in fact, when I was about five or six, Mom made a bargain with me - that she would give me five dollars if I could keep quiet for five minutes. Confident I could do so, I sat still and held my breath when the countdown began. After what seemed to me I had held my breath for hours, I thought I was going to pop like a balloon. Two minutes in, I exhaled and asked, "Is it five minutes yet Mom?" Wearily, she replied, "No Butch, it has only been two minutes." "But do I get my five dollars? It's almost been five minutes," I said. "Sure Butch, here's your five dollars," she replied shaking her head.

I enjoyed soul music and dancing growing up. Dancing came so naturally to me, as a youngster, I could do virtually every popular dance exceptionally well that the teenagers were doing on American Bandstand. Grown folks used to beg Mom to let me dance for them. In the early sixties, Chubby Checker didn't have anything on me when it came to doing the twist. When dancing, the world was my stage, and I loved being in the front and center of it. To say I was extroverted, would be an understatement.

I also found the world to be a curious place. I would ask questions ad nauseam in search of answers. To quench my inquisitive mind's thirst, Mom enrolled me in Elvinia's Kindergarten School when I turned four years old. It was owned, and operated, by a black woman who was known for enhancing kids' learning capabilities. Grown folks used to say, "Elvinia only takes the smart ones." The school, perhaps, catered to children who were slightly ahead of others. As I recall, Donald Charles, Marjorie Kirkland and I were the only four years old in the class of twenty or so students. When we turned five, the three of us were already doing first and second-grade level work. Although the school was structured in its approach, it was a lot of fun. It provided me with some of the answers my curious mind sought and fueled my eagerness to learn. Fridays were the best days because we got to watch a movie and eat popcorn and ice cream. My favorite films and television shows back then were cowboy pictures. Roy Rogers and The Lone Ranger were my favorites. Combine them with butter pecan ice cream, and I was in kid heaven.

When the school year wrapped up, we had a graduation ceremony replete with white caps and gowns. I'll never forget that day because Mom had bought me some new shoes for the occasion. The problem was, they were about one size too small. I walked around all day with my toes curled up to alleviate the pain. When we took our photo, I thought I was going to cry my feet hurt so much.

Kindergarten graduation with me in the middle

WESLEY CHAPEL

Growing up, Mom and I attended Wesley Chapel which was the oldest black Methodist Church in Arkansas. Per Wesley Chapel's website, the organization of Philander Smith College, occurred in the Church in 1867. This establishment explains to me the Church's connection with the College and why they are so close in proximity to one another. In 1968, the Church became affiliated with the United Methodist Church and was renamed Wesley Chapel United Methodist Church. I remember very well Mom's involvement in several activities related to the renaming.

Due to Mom's active participation in the Church, we were mainstays at Sunday service. On special occasions, Mom would sometimes be the "Keynote Speaker" or introduce the same. Mom was, at the time, the best public speaker I had ever seen. She was so well spoken that, whenever she spoke at Church, she would always receive a standing ovation afterward. I recall having to stay late after service, on more than one occasion, as a crowd of people would stand in line waiting to shake her hand and talk to her. This experience left an indelible impression on me. Mom was planting two "seeds" in my mind. The first was, "Notice son, how much research and preparation I do beforehand in getting ready to speak in public." The second was on developing and perfecting my public speaking skills by watching her firsthand.

I'm not sure at what age I got baptized at Wesley Chapel, but I do recall Easter egg hunts, Christmas services, and Communion. Oh, Communion! The children always took Communion together. We would eat broken pieces of saltine crackers and then drink Welch's Grape Juice. One Sunday, I happened to take Communion with Mom and the adults. As I drank the juice, I felt a burning sensation in my throat and gave out a big, "Ahh; that's good! Welch's Grape Juice!" The congregation roared with laughter. I'd never seen Mom that embarrassed. I could tell she wanted to find someplace to hide. As it turned out, the adults drank wine during Communion, and that was the first time I had ever tasted wine. Hence, my reaction, and the congregation's response. Mom started laughing, and all she could say was, "Butch, what in the world am I going to do with you?" Years later, Mom and I used to have some good laughs about that event.

Gibbs Elementary School

Gibbs Elementary

When I turned six, I entered first grade at Gibbs Elementary. The school was just one block away from our house on Cross Street. What was neat about where we lived was, as you looked out the front door, there was a football field with a surrounding track that separated Gibbs and Dunbar Junior High. There was also a Boys Club next to Gibbs, and a Community Center which had an indoor basketball court, football, and baseball fields. The closeness of these athletic venues was paradise for a kid like me who ate, drank and slept sports. It afforded me the opportunity to run, jump, hit, throw, slide and live out my sports fantasies.

My first day of school, Mom walked with me. I was excited to see neighbors standing at their doors, or outside on their porches waving me on, and wishing me good luck. It was like I was in a big parade. Surely, I had to be a "big boy" now because I was going to "big" school. When we arrived, Mom stopped at the Principal's office

38

to get directions to my classroom. As we walked up to the door of the room, I was ready to turn and run back home. Mom and my teacher convinced me, however, everything was going to be alright. Boy, were they right.

As I looked around the room, my six-year-old eyes saw "the most beautiful girl in the whole wide world." Her name was Peggy Sue Dean, and I was in love! I got to sit right behind Peggy Sue the first few weeks of school, but that ended abruptly when my teacher noticed one day how much time I was spending trying to talk to Peggy Sue. Subsequently, the teacher moved me to the middle aisle, middle seat of the classroom. No problem, there was always recess, and that gave me an opportunity to show off in front of Peggy Sue or learn some things about her. One was, she had a sister named Daisy. Whenever I would smile at Peggy Sue, she always smiled back. Surely this had to be love, my six-year-old mind thought.

Everything was going well in first grade until I fell on a rock playing football during recess one day. I broke my rib, and a sharp bone fragment pierced my skin. The doctor told my mother all he could do was wrap me up in tape, and let it heal on its own. When I returned to school the next day, the whole class wanted to see my rib. I kindly obliged. I pulled up my shirt and showed my bandaged rib with pride. Man, oh man, did I eat up the attention. I milked it long after the pain had subsided - which was a few days after the injury. You see, early on, I had already developed a flair for the dramatic.

My second and third-grade years were a blur with several exceptions. One being, Peggy Sue was suddenly gone. I didn't know if she and her family had moved away or not. It felt like she had vanished off the face of the earth. Another was, one day a call came over the intercom for our teacher to report to the Principal's Office. None of us knew why she had been called, but when she left out of the room, it was time to have some fun! We were dancing around, singing and throwing spitballs when our designated "teacher lookout" yelled, "She's coming!" Immediately, we settled down. Our teacher walked into the classroom crying and said, "President Kennedy has been assassinated." We were too young to know what the word meant, but we knew the President was dead. An eerie feeling engulfed the room. Everyone in the classroom began to cry. We were scared and sad. President Kennedy was a hero to many blacks back then. For me, he was in the category of Cassius Clay, good looking and famous. He had a lovely wife named Jackie, and their lives seemed like a fairy tale. On the day of the President's funeral, a television was placed in our classroom so we could watch the proceedings. As we watched, there was more tears and sadness that day.

There was one recess I will never forget. The bell rang for us to return to our classrooms. The boys broke out into a full sprint. Donald Charles and I were regarded as the fastest boys in our grade. The time had finally arrived to see who was the swiftest. The grass courtyard was full of students, so Donald and I were evading them as we were running. I was slightly ahead, and he was to my right when I took a glance to see where he was. When I turned my head to look straight ahead, a crowd of kids in front of me dispersed left and right. In a blink of an eye, I ran full speed into one of the iron tetherball poles and heard this loud "clang" just before I got knocked out cold. When I woke up, I was in bed at home with an icepack on the huge knot, the size of a golf ball, that was on my forehead. When I returned to school the next day, there was no sympathy from my classmates this time. Just a lot of jokes about the big knot on my head.

My fourth-grade teacher's name was Ms. Bussey. She was a very sweet lady whom the kids used to laugh at and talk about behind her back because of her weight. This discourtesy bothered me to no end because Mom had taught me not to tease or say bad things about people (i.e. a "seed.") One day I asked her, "What should I say when kids call Ms. Bussey fat?" She replied, "Tell them Ms. Bussey isn't fat, she's pleasingly plump." I tried it, and the "seed" Mom had given me worked. The kids pulled back on the insults. I did get labeled as the "class pet" though.

We had a kid in the class named Derek Person whom the girls thought was cute. He was the tallest kid in our classroom and reputed to be the toughest fourth grader in the school. Rumor had it he had beaten up a sixth-grader once. One day, Ms. Bussey got called to the Principal's office, and a big spitball fight broke out amongst the boys right after she left. I accidentally hit Derek with a whopper of a spitball, which he did not take kindly to. He was ready to fight. Although I was tough on the football field, I was deathly afraid of fighting. My inner fear was, if I ever got real mad, I might seriously hurt someone. I realized, if his fighting prowess was for real, I didn't stand much of a chance against Derek. I wasn't going to back down from him, however. It just wasn't in my nature. One of our classmates assumed the role of "teacher lookout" to warn us when Ms. Bussey was returning. The fight got underway, and Derek was all everyone said he was. I was holding my own though when suddenly the monitor yelled, "Here she comes!" At that very moment, Derek turned to look towards the door then back at me just as I was throwing a right-handed punch. It landed square on his chin, and he dropped like a tree. He was knocked out, and I was frightened out of my mind. I thought he was dead! Surely, the class was going to rat me out, and I would be in a world of trouble. Incredibly, it didn't happen. The class made up some cock-a-mamy story to Ms. Bussey like, "Derek had fallen out of his seat and hit his head" or something like that. After Ms. Bussey had brought Derek to his senses, he looked at me in disbelief about what had happened to him. Word quickly spread throughout the school about the fight, and suddenly I was viewed as a boxing hero. Neither Derek or anyone else knew it was a lucky punch and I sure didn't tell them - until now.

That year, the city of Little Rock had a spelling bee contest. Ms. Bussey nominated me to be Gibbs' fourth-grade representative. Growing up, Mom taught me how to break words down by how they sounded. We would play a game where she would say a word, and then I would have to enunciate it correctly, look it up in the dictionary, as fast as I could, and read aloud its definition. She would have me elongate my enunciation of the word to improve my articulation. I came to pride myself on being fast and correct with words and their spelling. The training (another "seed") paid dividends, and I won the city's fourth-grade spelling bee contest.

When I entered six grade, my math teacher was Mr. Johnson. He was a tall, slim, articulate, well-dressed man black man brimming with confidence. Unquestionably, he was my first male role model. I recall doing very well in Mr. Johnson's class, but there was one thing I consistently did that he didn't like. I talked incessantly. Thus, he gave me a C grade in conduct. I was devastated! It was the first time in my life I had received a grade other than an A or B. I didn't cry in class, but I poured a river of tears when I got home. I felt like I had failed, and let myself and my Mom down. As always, Mother was very encouraging about the event. She said to me something along the lines of, "Perhaps, Mr. Johnson sees something in you, and he is trying to teach you a lesson. Hopefully, you learned it. Don't worry; he just wants you to achieve your full potential. Just like me." I felt much better afterward, but man that "C" hurt.

Chapter 8

Hooked on Sports

For as long as I can remember, sports have played a vital role and been a large part of my life. I grew up loving sports. Inherently, sports provided me with various "seeds" of knowledge revolving around sportsmanship, teamwork, winning with dignity and losing gracefully, the benefit of hard work and sacrifice, plus humility to name some. Retrospectively, I shouldn't be surprised about why I was so fond of sports. Most of what I learned were just mere extensions of Mom's teachings.

Growing up, the Baltimore Colts were my favorite professional football team. I hated the Green Bay Packers and the Dallas Cowboys because they were my Colts' nemeses. As for college football, the Arkansas Razorbacks were the only team that existed or mattered to me. I lived and died with the Hogs, and despised the Texas Longhorns. On any given day, I could be the Colts' Johnny Unitas, Lenny Moore, Raymond Berry or Tommy McDonald. Sometimes, I would pretend to be my best friend's cousin, Jon Richardson, who was one of the first, if not the first, blacks to play football at Central High, and the first black scholarship football player at Arkansas. I could be Willie Mays or Jesse Owens or Walt Frazier or Curly Neal. I could be any athlete I wanted to be. I dreamed of being excellent at sports and becoming a professional athlete.

When I turned twelve years old, my athleticism began to stand out. I became one of those kids, everybody, it seemed, wanted to have on their team. I played tackle football every chance I got, and my reputation began to grow due to my combination of running ability, catching acumen and fundamentally sound tackling. We didn't have an organized tackle football team in the area, so the Community Center put together a flag football team that competed city-wide. As best as I can recall, Mr. Johnson was our Coach. On offense, I was a running back, and on defense, I played cornerback. The top players on our team were "June Bug" (an incredible athlete and our best player), his cousin "T.A.," and the "Twins" Jerry and Guerry. We won the city championship. In track, I competed in a city-wide 100-yard dash event. During the meet, I stumbled coming out of my stance and ended up finishing second to a kid in my neighborhood whom I routinely beat. I also became a starter on our 12-year old Pony League baseball team and began playing basketball for the first time.

My involvement in the sports I took part in was of my choosing or through the request of players and Coaches. Mom's ground rule with me was, I could play all the sports I wanted to, just as long as I brought home B grades or higher. Anything less, and I couldn't play - no ifs ands or buts about it! Talk about a motivator! The good thing for me was, I was above average in school and sports so, it didn't turn out to be a problem. I knew Mom meant every word she said, though.

I find it interesting that it was Mom who got me involved in basketball. Whether it was out of circumstance, her intuition or both, I'm glad she did. I used to watch, fixated, NBA games on Sunday. During timeouts, and when my Mom wasn't around or looking, I would dribble a tennis ball and shoot in wastebaskets throughout the house. I'd mainly watched the New York Knicks (my favorite team), Boston Celtics (I hated them), the Philadelphia 76'ers, and the Los Angeles Lakers. Walt "Clyde" Frazier of the Knicks was my favorite player. He was one cool brother; a snappy dresser with a sharp goatee, smooth jump shot and fancy behind the back passes. I pretended to be him.

One Saturday afternoon, out of nowhere, Mom suggested I go over to the Community Center to play basketball and work on my game. I thought it was an odd recommendation considering I'd never played the game. Subsequently, I went over to the Center and played basketball for the first time in my life. I liked it, and while it was fun, I was terrible at it. Primary reasons being, my shot was horrific, and I had a hard time shooting over taller players. Strange thing, though, I had an uncanny ability when it came to dribbling a basketball. It just came naturally to me. It was as if the ball and my hands were in sync with one another. "How could I go from dribbling a tennis ball to an object as large as a basketball so effortlessly?" I wondered. It made no sense at all to me. Even with this newfound skill, I wasn't hooked on the game as I was with football.

A few days later, I confided to Mom; I had noticed many of peers were growing and getting bigger than me. I told her if I didn't have a growth spurt, football might not be a choice for me down the road due to my lack of size. I talked about my love for the sport, how good I was at it, and did not know what I'd do without football. A few days later, Mom came home from work, and said, "Butch, come go with me." I had no idea where we were headed to in the cab outside. The driver took us to Philander Smith where the Panthers basketball team had a game that night.

Philander Smith had a small guard who immediately caught my eye during the b-ball game. He was mesmerizing. I could relate to him because he was small in stature like me. The little Panther could dribble, shoot, defend and was easily the best player on the floor. Mom said to me, "Butch, do you know who that is?" My reply was, "No Ma'am, but he sure is good." She said, "He's an All-American. If football doesn't work out for you, maybe this is a sport for you to consider. If you work at it, who knows, you might get pretty good at it." I was so impressed with the small player, I went to the gym the very next day, and didn't stop going back. I was hooked on the game.

At the urging of friends, I also started playing baseball more often. Truth be told, I didn't care much about baseball initially. I thought it was boring and too slow. In my mind, it was something to keep me busy, however, until football season rolled back around. Instinctively, I could field, chase down fly balls, and steal bases. Hitting was another matter. From the very beginning, I had a fear of getting hit in the head with the ball. It didn't make sense considering I had been playing tackle football for six years without a helmet. My anxiety when batting caused me to "bail out" slightly or in baseball vernacular "step in the bucket." This means, as a right-handed batter, my left foot (i.e. "stride" foot) would pull towards shortstop instead of towards the pitcher, as it should. The result caused me to open my left shoulder and hips when I swung. The net effect was, I would be late to the baseball when I swung. That summer of 1968, some of my friends asked me to try out for our local Pony League baseball team for which they were already playing. "Why, not! What the heck," I thought. After trying out at second base and the outfield, I made the squad. One day at practice our Coach, nicknamed Chin, was hitting hard ground balls to the infielders, particularly our third baseman. The poor guy was struggling with the blistering baseballs coming his way. Coach Chin moved me to third and said, "Butch, there's a reason why third base is called the hot spot!" Afterward, he started hitting missiles my way. I didn't back down. Maybe it was my football mentality, but my premise that day was, "Nothing is getting past me, by me, or through me. I'm making all the plays!" Following, I became our third baseman, but that didn't last long.

We had a short, bowlegged first baseman, nicknamed "Little Sam," who was an absolute phenom. One practice, Coach hit me a ground ball which I backhanded and threw very high to first base. The ball had to have been close to 2 feet over Little Sam's head. I thought for sure it was going to land on the street. Little Sam jumped up in the

48

air, caught the ball and landed in a full split with his right foot on the outer part of the bag. I was thinking to myself, "That's impossible!" If I hadn't seen it with my own eyes, I wouldn't have believed the play. I guess I had a deer in headlights look on my face when teammates told me, "Oh, he does that all of the time." I was thinking, "No way! Man, if we can hit a bit, this team is going to be something!" To this day, I still can't believe the play.

Out of necessity, I wound up playing catcher. What happened was, our starter got called up to play on our local 14-year-old Pony League team, and no one on our squad wanted to play catcher, due to its rigorous demands. That practice, I told Coach Chin I would give it a shot. The first time I put on the gear, it didn't take long to figure out I was "bat-blind." I would blink my eyes when a batter was swinging and lose track of where the ball was going. My debut was going terrible, and just before Coach was about to take me out from behind the plate and try someone else, I said, "Give me one more try." I made up my mind to not blink my eyes and to track the ball all the way into my mitt. Instantly, I began tracking pitches during a swing and backhanding balls in the dirt. After that, I was our catcher.

When there weren't enough kids to play with outside, I would head over to the Boys Club for some billiards and trampoline jumping. I became good at both. I used to beat the older guys in shooting pool to the extent they came up with a scam in which I was the bait. Here's how it worked. When a new guy would come into the Club to play pool, the older guys would give me a signal and bring the newbie over to watch me play. I would play poorly, and the older guys would wager the new guy that I could beat him. The poor sap would bite every time, and I'd beat him unmercifully. While the older men profited, all I got was a lot of free candy! Goodness knows Mom would have killed me if she'd known what I'd been doing.

On a trampoline, I could do challenging routines such as double backward and forward somersaults and land standing or in a layout. I had one move where I would do a flip and hit the roof of the Club with my feet. One day I was showing off and landed face first and hit my mouth on an unpadded piece of the trampoline's steel bar. Blood was going everywhere, and my permanent tooth was dangling from my gum. I ran home with my hand over my mouth to catch the blood, and my tooth which I was sure was going to fall out. I don't remember much about my visit to the Dentist, but incredibly, he managed to save the tooth. That ended my trampoline jumping.

Chapter 9

Remembering Akron

Every summer, from the time I was four or five years old, Mom would fly me to Akron, Ohio to visit Grandma (Eula Mae Nevels), Granddad (Earl Nevels) and my cousins Allen and Tony Mitchell whom my Grandparents raised as Legal Guardians. I loved being in Akron during the summers. These regular visits were Mom's way, I feel, of keeping me connected to family and ensuring I was exposed to things outside of just Little Rock. This "seed" implied, "Expose yourself to new people and new places because by doing so it will broaden you as a person and your perceptions." Other relatives who lived in Akron were my Great Uncle, Walter Brown (Grandma's brother) and his wife Great Aunt Emma, who lived down the street. Tony, Allen and I (i.e. the "trio") called them Auntie and Uncle. Grandma's son, my Uncle Clarence Brown and his wife Aunt Mable, resided in another area of town, as did their adult children, Cousins Barbara and Eddie Brown. Another cousin, Diedre Brown, also lived in another part of the city.

Looking back, my visits to Akron helped me to become more well-rounded. I had to learn how to get along with people who weren't in my usual social sphere. Plus, the environment also caused me to be aware of my diction because it seemed everyone in Akron spoke well, irrespective of their level of academic attainment. Take Lebron James

51

for instance. He's a high school graduate from Akron and if you notice he speaks quite well. That was what I was exposed to during the 2+ years I lived in Akron during the summers.

When I visited Akron the summer of 1969, Allen had turned 15, Tony 14, and I was 13. To me, they were the brothers I never had. We were all outgoing and athletic. We enjoyed doing things together, such as playing sports, swimming, riding bikes, skating and boy we could run! Allen was the fastest and best athlete of the "trio." He was a burgeoning football and track star in Akron, and he would go on to earn a track scholarship to Kent State. Tony was the second fastest, then me. In addition to being a phenomenal athlete, Allen was good looking, a straight A student and quite popular with the girls. He had a red afro that would match the Jackson 5 and was the first black person I had met who had freckles. I looked up to my "big brother." Tony was every bit as charismatic as his brother. He had a charming smile and dimples which the girls adored. Tony also played the drums, no small feat considering my cousin his right thumb at an early age. Without question, he was the coolest and best dressed of the three of us.

I loved Grandma almost as much as I loved Mom. Today, I understand better why I felt for her so. The "seeds of knowledge" she passed down to Mom were passed down to me. The two women's values and belief systems were virtually identical. Grandma was an amazing woman who was deeply rooted in the Lord. She attended Centenary United Methodist Church and served on the Usher Board.

It wasn't unusual for her to, at the spur of a moment, put on a Mahalia Jackson gospel album and just hum along. Whenever Grandma contemplated something or was worried, she would unconsciously interlock her fingers and twiddle her thumbs. For some reason, this always fascinated me. When it rained, and there was lightning, Grandma would have Allen, Tony, and I find a place to sit still and be quiet, because "The Lord is at work." she'd say.

My Grandmother was the best cook I have ever been around. There's no doubt in my mind; she would have been wealthy if she had opened a restaurant or a catering business. To say her meals were pleasing to the palate would be an understatement. She used to make a salad dish comprised of cucumbers, onions, and vinegar that I particularly liked. In addition to her meals, her desserts were, as a former manager of mine used to say, "To die for!"

At that time, Akron was known as the "Rubber Capital of the World." Four of the nation's five largest tire companies were headquartered there. Goodyear, Firestone, B.F. Goodrich and General Tire were the economic engines that drove the city. Grandma worked as a domestic for the Firestone family. Whenever their children would outgrow clothes, their parents would "hand them down" to Grandma. Goodness knows Tony, Allen, and I was wearing Polo and Izod shirts and shorts long before they became trendy.

Granddad was a bald headed, dark skinned, built like a rock man who had served in World War II and was a foreman at Goodyear. He had an intimidating look about him and a deep baritone voice that would put fear in a man. His voice was so deep, to this day, I believe I heard him from two blocks away, as I swam underwater, roar, "Tony, Butch!" to let the two of us know, it was time to come home. Some of his idiosyncrasies were: He would always criticize people's driving, which I thought was hilarious because you could hear him burning rubber with his tires when he made a turn two blocks away onto Diagonal Road. Afterward, he would pull into the driveway, stop on the edge of the pavement and spin his tires to cause the gravel rocks to fly onto the sidewalk. Invariably, one or more of the 'trio" would be called outside to sweep the strewn rocks back into the driveway.

Another oddity of his was, he would refer to people as a "Dirty Louse" if they did or said something he didn't agree with or like. Another one, which I didn't like, was after cutting the grass, Allen, Tony and I would have to edge the lawn with hand clippers or scissors. I always thought this was strange and felt it was punishment for something. The funniest thing Granddad would do occurred on every Sunday without fail. We knew Granddad hadn't been to church, but when he picked Grandma and the "trio" up from Sunday service, he would be dressed to the nines, as if he had been to church. He would sport an Adolph Hitler-like mustache he'd created using Grandma's eyebrow pencil. It was hilarious and would bring me, Allen, and Tony to tears.

My grandparents lived on Noble Avenue across the street from Crouse Elementary School, which had a gymnasium, playground, baseball field (the outfield was also used for football), and a basketball court. Like the layout in Little Rock, this nearby environment was conducive to my athletic development. Their house was multi-level, with a screened-in porch. The basement had a bar, laundry area, bathroom with shower and sitting room where Tony practiced playing his drums. Grandma had a white tub washing machine with rollers and a hand crank. After washing a load of clothes, she would put them through the rollers and turn the crank to wring out the water in the clothes. She used to use Argo starch for our clothes, and in addition to ironing them, she would iron our underwear. Grandma was "old school." The main floor of the house had a living room, dining room, and kitchen. The second floor had two bedrooms, where my grandparents and Allen slept, a full bath, kitchen and sitting room. The attic had been converted into two bedrooms, one of which was rented out to a tenant named Gladys Harris who the "trio" refer to as "Aunt Gladys." To this day, Aunt Gladys remains one of the nicest ladies I've ever met. The additional bedroom was where Tony and I slept.

Picking cherries during the summer was one of my favorite activities. Most of the cherry trees in the surrounding neighborhood grew the red version of the fruit. There were some houses, however, near Auntie and Uncle's, where the trees produced the sweet, dark purple, buckeye cherry. Homeowners usually tried to protect them from being picked and eaten by ravenous kids such as Allen, Tony and me. There's nothing like taking home a bag full of cherries, washing them, and then putting a smidgen of sugar on them before indulging.

Tony and Allen's Dad, "Uncle Mitch" would come by the house to check in on us. One day, we were on the football field, and he challenged us to a 40-yard dash race. The "trio" laughed because we surely thought there was no way this "old man" was going to beat us. The four of us got down in our track stance, and I called the start. "On your mark, get set, ready, go!" I yelled. Allen and Uncle Mitch started out even. As Allen began to pull away from him, Tony started pulling away from me. The order of finish was Allen, Uncle Mitch, Tony, then me. We were in total disbelief as to Uncle Mitch's speed. I said to my cousins, "Man, your Dad is fast. I see where you guys get your speed from."

Granddad was a huge baseball fan. To illustrate, he used to make Allen, Tony and I watch the Cleveland Indians play. It wouldn't have been so bad, were it not for the fact the Indians were the worst team in Major League Baseball at the time. It was excruciating watching them. There was a bright side with Granddad and baseball that summer, though. He taught me a lot about playing the position of catcher. He taught me how to get out of my crouch quickly on bunts and stolen base attempts. Granddad showed me how to block balls with me chest protector to keep them in front of me. He also taught me how to trash talk to a batter to get in his head. Things like, "You can't hit it if you can't see it," or "You're going to break your bat because the label is facing the ball" or "Watch out for my pitcher. This guy is wild. He's probably going to hit you." "Anything to annoy the batter or get him distracted," Granddad said.

Amazed by his baseball knowledge, I asked Granddad if he had ever played the game. He replied, "Oh, yeah." As he reminisced, he confided, "I was a catcher like you back in the day. I was damn good, and boy did I talk a lot of trash behind the plate. One day, I made this kid named Josh Gibson so mad, he hit me on the head with his bat. It knocked all the hair off my head. That's why I'm bald!" I bought the hairless part, hook line, and sinker. Hey, I was thirteen years old and didn't know about male patterned baldness. Years later, when I heard about the exploits of Josh Gibson in the Negro Leagues, and that he had supposedly hit more homers than Babe Ruth, I remembered the first time I had ever heard Gibson's name was from my Granddad. So, knowledgeable about baseball was he; it was reasonable for me to assume Granddad had played at a high level in his day. Curious, as to if he had played professionally, several years ago, I researched former Negro League players to see if Granddad's name was listed. I couldn't find him, but I imagine he had played against Gibson in a barnstorming game.

Four things happened to me in sports that summer I will never forget. In basketball, I was getting much better. I could hold my own against Ricky L. who was the best player in my age group in the area. We'd play one on one, and I could see myself improving by the day. Allen took notice and shared with me one day, "Butch, you're getting good at this."

One day, some neighborhood boys and I were receiving football instruction from former Ohio State All-American running back and NFL first-round draft pick, Don Clark. I made a diving, full layout catch that caught his eye. Next, I caught a ball over my head beyond my right shoulder one handed, then tip-toed the sideline and outraced my defender for a touchdown. Coach Clark stopped the session and pulled me over in front of all the kids. He asked me my name, where I was from, my team and Coach's name. After answering his questions, he said, "You've got the best hands I've ever seen on a kid your age." After thanking him, I told him I might have to give up the sport if I didn't start growing. He replied, "It would be a shame if you gave it up." Allen ran into Don Clark in 2016 and told him I had recently been in Akron for Aunt Eloise's (Allen and Tony's Mother) funeral. Incredibly, Don still remembered me and said to Allen, "How could I ever forget him!"

Akron held its 10th annual Junior Olympics event that summer. Tony, Allen, me and kids from the neighborhood competed for Crouse Elementary. I made it to Crouse's "Gold Glove" boxing championship finals and went up against J.M., an eleven-year-old who threw me "the catch" I made in front of Don Clark. J.M. was the toughest guy, in my age group, in the area. He was Mike Tyson before Mike Tyson and looked like him too. The first time I saw Tyson on television, I thought he was from Akron and was J.M.'s son! I broke up a fight once between J.M. and a tough 14-year-old when he started beating up the guy unmercifully. I think he broke the kid's nose because blood was going everywhere. In the preliminary rounds of the boxing tournament, J.M. had knocked out every one of his opponents! He and I were to meet in the finals.

Cognizant, I couldn't go toe-to-toe with J.M., my strategy was to emulate my favorite boxer, Muhammad Ali. I had to stay on my toes in the middle of the ring, throw jabs, and circle to my left to decrease a hard right-handed punch from my opponent. Plus, for my life and safety's sake, I had to stay the heck off the ropes! My strategy was, and to paraphrase, "Float like a butterfly and sting like a bee," to keep from getting knocked out. My goal was to win on points. Former World Light Heavyweight Champion Archie Moore officiated the three-round championship bout. It was cool having him in the ring. My strategy against J.M. was working until the third round when I got caught up in a corner against the ropes. He came in for "the kill." I managed to duck, bob and weave and get away unscathed, thank God. I ended up winning on points. I thought J.M. was going to kill me afterward, but he didn't. Fortunately for me, he and I always got along well, thank goodness.

Our Crouse track team usually dominated the summer Junior Olympics. That year was no exception. The team set multiple records on the day. Allen defeated a kid rumored to be Jesse Owens' nephew, in the 220-yard dash semifinals. Before the race, people from across town predicted Owens' supposed nephew would win. I assured them, once Allen hit the curve the race would be over. Sure enough, it happened just like I called it. As I recall, Allen pulled a hamstring during the semifinals and didn't compete in the finals. Tony took first place in the 14-15-year-old boy's triple jump with a leap of 34' 7 ¼", and third place in the 100-yard dash. J.M., T.S., R.M. and I won the

200-yard shuttle relay in a time of 26.3 seconds. Crouse's girl's team was spectacular as well. Crouse took first place overall and claimed 20 medals (13-first place, 3-second place, and 4-third place) on the day.

While I didn't get into too much trouble that summer, I did get into a fight with a kid named Victor. I accidentally hit him with a horseshoe when he inexplicably ran across the tossing area. He ended up pummeling me under the big oak tree on Crouse's playground. My right knee, which I had scraped badly stealing a base in baseball, started bleeding when Victor and I were tussling on the ground. Beforehand, Grandma had told me not to do anything to reinjure the knee. Beaten to a frazzle, I walked home with blood flowing down my leg and knowing I had to face Grandma.

Eula Mae Nevels didn't approve of the "trio" fighting. Therefore, I knew I was going to be in deep trouble with her for doing so. When she saw my appearance, Grandma asked me what had happened. I told her, and she remarked, "Number one, I said no fighting." Now was not the time for me to point out to her, Uncle Clarence, her son, was a former professional fighter, so, I didn't bring that up. "Two, I told you not to mess up that knee, didn't I?" "Yes Ma'am," I replied. She went on to say, "Now you can go back and do to him what I'm about to do you, or you can go get me three switches right now!" Faced with the prospect of having to deal with a whipping from Grandma or Victor; I chose Victor.

As I walked back across the baseball field, Victor laughed and said, "I can't believe you came back for more. I'm gonna kick your

60

a#$!" I had other intentions, however. Motivated by the fear of getting a whipping from Grandma, I beat Victor to a pulp! After proudly walking in to share my conquest with her, Grandma said, "Now go outside and get me three branches. Peel the leaves off them, and then I'm going to show you how to braid them." "But Grandma, I won," I said. "Doesn't matter. I told you not to be fighting in the first place. Now go get me those branches and don't bring back little ones." Talk about a confused kid as I walked to the hedge bushes! "To fight, or not to fight," was my big question. Up until then, Grandma had never laid a hand on me. Now, I was about to pick out my own branches for the butt whipping of my life.

We sat in the kitchen, and Grandma taught me how to braid three branches. Next, we went upstairs to her bedroom, and she closed the door. My heart was in my throat. "Pull your pants down. Now Butchie, this is going to hurt me more than it's going to hurt you." "Yeah, right!", I remember thinking. After getting the spanking of my life, Grandma felt so bad about the whipping; she showered me with love. I didn't hesitate to rub in my elevated position with Allen and Tony. I got to eat all the ice cream I wanted, and I let my "brothers" know it by golly! I could mess up, and Grandma would overlook my mistake. I would laugh at my cousins when they were admonished for theirs. I didn't take this period of enhanced kindness from Grandma to lightly, though, because I had seen the "dead end," no pun intended, of me making her mad.

I guess I didn't learn my lesson with my Grandmother. For some reason, Tony and I started this thing whereby we would urinate through the screen of our bedroom window, onto the second-floor roof of the house. "Heck, it's quicker than walking down the stairs to the bathroom to pee," we must have been thinking. Inevitably, Grandma came up to our room to see if Tony and I we were up to any mischief. As she walked around, she started sniffing the air. Finally, she said, "What's that funny smell? I smell something. What is that I'm smelling?" Tony and I, with guilt written all over our faces, were like, "I don't know. I don't smell anything." As Grandma, moved closer to the window, Tony's and my life flashed before us. "You boys been peeing out this window? I know you boys haven't been peeing out this window!" I am pleased to report; Tony and I are still alive. I got off easier than he did because I was still wounded from my last encounter with Grandma. Poor Tony, I didn't think my Cousin was going to survive. He and I still laugh about that to this day.

One day, the "trio," led by ringleader Allen, had this bright idea to go to Victor's next door neighbor's house to pick buckeye cherries off the tree without asking. The owner of the house probably had the biggest and plumpest buckeye cherries in the neighborhood. We climbed his backyard fence and scampered up the tree. We had a ball eating and picking the delicious fruit. Allen convinced Tony and me the sweetest cherries were higher up in the tree. We bought it hook, line and sinker. Typically, the bigger, juicier and more delicious cherries are lower on a tree. One could easily tell because the branches tended to bend the most. Allen made hay with this knowledge and kept encouraging Tony and me to keep climbing higher and higher. Out of nowhere, out came the homeowner brandishing a garden hose. Allen scrambled down the tree and was gone in a flash. Tony got to a point where he could jump down from the tree. When he landed, the owner whacked Tony a good one on the back with the hose. I had to come down from near the top of the tree. Preoccupied with Tony, I managed to escape Victor's neighbor unharmed. The three of us never went back there again that summer. I didn't know it at the time, but that would be my last summer vacation in Akron.

When I attended Aunt Eloise's funeral, I had a chance to see many of the friends I grew up with in Akron. Our memories flowed. I spent time with Janice and Linda Lewis and their Mom (Bea). I also saw John Dyer (J.D.) Jr., and his brother Delbert, Big Harp or Harper as some call him, Kenny Hilliard, Alabama, Aunt Gladys, Cousin Diedre and others. I will always remember my times in Akron with fondness.

Chapter 10

Dunbar Junior High

I started attending Dunbar Junior High the fall of 1969. The school was right across the street from the brick duplex house Mom, and I had moved into on Cross Street, and just a block down from our old house. When I crossed the street, I would be at the steps leading up to Dunbar's gymnasium. I used to ride my bike around the large oval which was between the gym and the school's cafeteria, pretending I was in a stock car race. Dunbar was an expansive multi-level building resembling historic Central High. I've learned the resemblance is no coincidence. The two schools were built two years apart by the same architectural firm.

Dunbar Junior High   Central High

Dunbar, which had previously been the feeder school to Horace Mann High, was solid academically, had an award-winning band and was the perennial state champion in basketball. We had tremendous school spirit and pride at Paul Lawrence Dunbar Junior

High, and students knew they were a part of something very special going on. I remember well, the tremendous feeling I had walking the halls of the Collegiate Gothic and Art Deco designed school.

It wasn't difficult for me to get acclimated to Dunbar because most of its students had attended Gibbs Elementary. I jumped right in and was very active at the school. I made the seventh-grade football team - the Dunbar Mighty Mites and the symphonic band as a third seat, first chair trumpet player. It was unheard of for a seventh-grader to achieve the prestigious "first chair" position at the school. Two other seventh-graders also did it that year. One was a flutist, the other a clarinetist. I also played Marc Antony in, "Julius Caesar" before the entire student body. Mom assisted me daily in preparing for my role, which would be my first public speaking event. She had me break out sections of what I was to recite, to make the memorization easier. She advised I practice each section no less than four times so the words would flow naturally. When I asked Mom for suggestions on what I could do to combat my nerves when looking out at the crowd, she recommended I look right over their heads, like she did when speaking in public, and focus on an object on the back wall such as a clock or picture. Once I became comfortable, she said; then I could begin to peruse the audience with my eyes and look right into theirs. This sage advice proved invaluable during my future public speaking engagements and throughout my corporate career. After the play, the cast and I were roundly applauded. When I took my bow, I received a standing ovation. Lastly, I made the seventh-grade basketball team.

Suffice it to say; these accomplishments made me well known in the school.

In the fall, the band played in the stands during Varsity football games. One game a white school was beating the Varsity soundly and their Coach rubbed it in by running up the score. Band members were as about as upset as our players and Coaches. I told my peers, "Don't worry; we'll get them when basketball season comes around. Dunbar never forgets!" When the schools met during basketball season, our Varsity Head Basketball Coach left the starters in the entire game. We won by about 50 points it seemed. Dunbar didn't forget and made its point!

On the Mighty Mites football team, I made first string at running back. T.A., June Bug, and the Twins also made the team and were first string. Our first game, we played a white school that was supposed to have the most dominant junior high football program in the city. On Dunbar's first play from scrimmage, I took the handoff and ran between the left guard and tackle. I accelerated through a slight gap, then faked inside and went outside on a linebacker. When I turned upfield, near the sideline, I saw nothing but green grass in front of me. I thought to myself, "I'm going to score!" About 20 yards into my run, I made a crucial mistake and looked up in the stands for my Mom, while the play was still going on. I saw my Mother jumping up and down gleefully then suddenly she put her hands over her eyes and said, "Oh no!" Just as I turned my head to look back up field, their safety nearly decapitated me. I went flying out of bounds and landed face-first in a puddle of mud. To this day, I don't know where in the world the guy came from. When I got up, there was mud all in my face mask. As I was wiping it off, I looked at Mom and thought she was going to faint. Woozy from the hit, I went back to the huddle mumbling to myself, "Rule number one. Never look up in the stands. Rule number two. Never forget about their safety!" We ended up beating our opponent so soundly, every school in our league took us off their schedule.

With no teams willing to play us, Mr. Johnson and some other men in the community gathered together to try to figure out what to do about the dilemma. We started back practicing every day at the YMCA, which was about four blocks from where Mom and I lived. The practices were so intense; you'd have thought we were preparing for the Super Bowl. Still, no one would play us. We learned, teams felt we had kids older than 13-years of age (the seventh-grade limit), and were competing with ineligible players. We felt cheated by the accusation. We were all the proper age. T.A.'s birthday, however, as I recall, was right on the age limit deadline or the day after. He was the only player that could have been in question.

One practice, a new kid, showed up. I had never seen him or heard about him before. His nickname was Cherokee and man, oh man, could he hit. He hit harder than June Bug, me or one of the Twins who I thought was our hardest hitter. Cherokee was a tackling machine! One day, we ran a drill where the linebackers had to practice catching the football. The exercise was designed to get them accustomed to catching the ball in the event it got tipped in the air and came their way during a game. The Coaches told us not to go full speed. Well, all I knew was full speed. Cherokee ran a pass route across the middle, and I hit him with everything I had. My teammates looked at me as if I was crazy for hitting him so hard. Several of them said, "Butch, he's going to kill you when it's your turn to run the drill." When my turn came, Cherokee hit me so hard; I flipped 360° in the air and saw my feet fly by with the sky as a backdrop. I landed so hard the wind got knocked out of me. Hurt and humiliated, I got up and headed home. The Coaches asked me where I was going. I snapped back, "I quit! Cherokee is crazy!"

Walking home, I cried because I knew by quitting; I had let myself, my teammates, Coaches, and Mom down. In my day, most black Coaches wouldn't allow a "quitter" to come back. I had let my pride cause me to walk away from the sport I loved most. A few days passed, and my phone rang. It was one of the Twins. He said, excitedly, "Butch, we've got a game!" I replied, "Man, that's great. Who are you guys playing?" He said, "We're playing Horace Mann's seventh-grade team!" I said, "You're kidding me. Horace Mann? That's going to be a huge game. Tell the guys I said, good luck." The Twin paused and said, "The reason why I'm calling is, the Coaches and players wanted you to come back to the team." I couldn't believe my ears. I told Twin I would be at the next practice. The next day when I arrived, I was welcomed back with open arms. Our Head Coach

informed me I was being moved to wide receiver for the game against
Horace Mann to take advantage of my pass catching ability.

THE BIG GAME

We practiced harder than we ever had in preparation for our
crosstown rival. There was a "Us versus Them" mentality in the air; it
seemed, amongst blacks in both communities stemming from Dunbar
students now being zoned to the "white" Central High versus our old
feeder school, the "black" Horace Mann High. As the game neared, it
felt to me as if our crosstown brethren viewed the game as, "The real
blacks who remained loyal to their community versus those "***sellouts***"
who went with those white folks over at Central High."

Horace Mann's team had gone undefeated during the season.
The buzz around the city was, not only was the team incredible; it had
a superstar player named Bar-B-Q. The day of the game, our players
and Coaches met at the Community Center around 9 A.M. for the
"Showdown at Noon." Our team knew the game was big, but we had
no idea how big. Our first clue came when we walked into the gym.
There were cots on the floor everywhere. The next clue was, parents
had laid out a spread of food for us on tables. That's when we realized;
this was no typical 13-year-old football game. For the first time in my
life, I had butterflies in my stomach.

Our Head Coach laid out our game plan. He said we had one job and only one job to do. That was to stop their top player, the kid named Bar-B-Q. "11 men to the ball every time he touches it!" our Head Coach implored. We left the Community Center and headed over to Dunbar's field. When we arrived, the field was jam packed with fans. They were at least 2 to 3 people deep on each side. As we walked by, we could see people betting money on the game. No doubt this was going to be an absolute war.

We won the toss and chose to receive the ball. June Bug and I were the kick returners. Before the kickoff, our Head Coach told the two of us he wanted me to return the ball. On the kickoff, the ball was coming right to me. Inexplicably, June Bug cut me off, caught the ball, and ran up the middle of the field. Bar-B-Q hit him so hard it sounded like a gun had gone off. The hit was so devastating when June Bug bent over in the huddle afterward, a single tear hung on one of his eyelashes. June Bug was one tough customer, a man amongst boys, who never cried. By no means was he crying. He had just been hit so hard; it caused a tear gland to secrete. I remember thinking, "Man, I'm glad I didn't catch the ball!" The "War" was on!

The game was as hard hitting as we imagined it would be. We "gang tackled," 11 men to the ball, every time Bar-B-Q touched it. We were challenging their quarterback to beat us with the pass. On one play, Bar-B-Q took a handoff up the middle and Cherokee hit him so hard you could hear the players on both teams go "Wow!" Two hard hitting warriors collided at the same time. It was something to see.

Throughout the game, neither team could move the ball nor had they gone past midfield. T.A. called for a pass on one play, but was under a heavy pass rush and didn't see I was wide open. I noticed when I ran my pass route, a fake slant then "out" pattern, my defender had been completely fooled with the move. When I got back to the huddle, I told T.A. what happened and asked for him to call the play again. As a rule of thumb, only the quarterback is supposed to talk in the huddle, and T.A. sternly reminded me of such. Two more times I came back to the huddle and said, "T.A., I've got my guy beat. Call the play; I'll be wide open." Both times T.A. said, "Butch, shut up!" A few plays later, he relented and called for the route. The play worked to perfection. After faking out my defender, I was wide open on the right sideline. I caught the pass and turned up the field looking to score. This time I didn't forget about the safety, but I still got leveled by him. We were past midfield, and our fans were going nuts. I saw Coach Chin on the sideline going crazy. I also saw adults increasing their bets on the game after my catch.

Now that we were across midfield, and having seized momentum, we began to run the ball down Horace Mann's throat. One of the Twins had most of the carries. Ultimately, we reached the 1-yard line, and T.A. called for a run play off the right tackle. I moved to tight end on the play and threw a block that knocked my man down the hill leading to the side door of Dunbar's gymnasium. The Twin ran right off my butt and scored. We missed the extra point but closed out the game with a 6-0 win. We had gone undefeated at 2-0 and were the City Champs in the eyes of many in the black community.

BASKETBALL TRYOUTS

Dunbar held its basketball tryouts that late fall. I was nervous, and I had reason to be. First, I had never played organized basketball before and second; I was trying out for the best Junior High School basketball program in the state of Arkansas. The odds of making Dunbar's prestigious team were slim for anyone. Add to the mix, my lack of height and my rawness in basketball; I was faced with a daunting task. I had three things going for me, though. They were: my athleticism, dribbling ability, and motivation from seeing Philander Smith's small All-American player.

A few days into the tryouts, I suffered a slight fracture to my left index finger. Although it was painful, I persevered and ended up making the team. I was thrilled. June Bug also made the team. He got pulled up to the Varsity during tryouts after our ninth-grade Head Coach saw him dunk during a scrimmage. To my knowledge, previously only two other seventh-graders had made Varsity in the history of the school.

When the basketball team was announced over the school's intercom, chills ran down my spine. When you played basketball for Dunbar, you were treated like royalty, and a lot of people in the school

72

and community knew who you were. Especially, the girls. I don't think it was a coincidence I met my first girlfriend shortly after the basketball team was announced.

Chapter 11

Life Changing Event

My life growing up in Little Rock was like a fairy tale. It was as if I was living a dream and nothing could go wrong. Until one fateful night. I had been running around playing sports all day, and I was totally exhausted. So much so, I slept on the bottom bunk of my bunk bed, which I had only done once before. I was coming out of a deep sleep when I heard a crying sound. Disoriented, I heard it again, and said, "Mom is that you, crying? What's wrong? I'll be right there." I turned on the light switch, but the light didn't come on. The bulb must have blown, I thought. The house was pitch black, but I knew its configuration so well I could navigate the rooms with my eyes closed. When Mom heard me in the hall, she yelled, "Butch, don't move. Don't take a step further. He's got a gun to my head! He said he'd kill me if you come in here." Without thinking or hesitating, I said, "Mom, I'm coming!" I ran up the hall and bumped into someone who ran out the back door. When I got to Mom, she was frightened out of her mind and crying uncontrollably. As I comforted her, I remember saying something like, "It's alright Mom, I'm here now. I've got you. I'm not going to let anyone hurt you. Just stop your crying now. It's going to be alright."

After she had calmed down a little bit, I told Mom, I was going to call the police. She cried out, "No, No, don't call the police. He said he'd kill you if you did." I replied, "Mom, I've got to call them. I'm going to call them right now." Mom begged me not to. Just as I was about to pick up the phone to call the police, it rang. I said, "Hello." There was total silence. I hung up the phone and got ready to dial again. It rang again. I said, "Hello." Total silence again. The third time the phone rang, I said, "I'm going to find out who you are and I'm going to kill you!" The phone continued to ring all night. I took Mom to her bed and laid beside her. I stayed awake all night with my wood baseball bat in my hand.

The next morning, I remained by Mom's side until I felt she was doing well enough for me to leave her alone for a little while. I told her I was going outside and would be back shortly. She had no idea what I was planning. Mom didn't have to say a word to me about what happened that night. My instincts told me all I needed to know, and I was totally pissed! As I walked out the back door and locked it, I had one thing and one thing only on my mind. I was going to find the son of a bitch that hurt my Mom and kill him!

I polled some of my friends to see if there was anyone new in the neighborhood. I must have talked to about a dozen people to no avail. I decided to head home to check on Mom. I was about thirty yards from the house when I came across a friend. I asked him if there was anyone new in the neighborhood, and he said, "Oh yeah, Butch. There's this guy that just got out of jail or prison or something. He's staying with the people who live right in front of me, just across from you."

I walked in the back door of our rented house and went to Mom's bedroom to check on her. She was asleep, or so I thought. I crept into the kitchen and opened the drawer where Mom kept her butcher's knives. I picked up the largest knife and tiptoed to the back door. As I grabbed the knob, I heard from behind me, "Butch, where are you going with that knife?" I said, "I found out where the guy lives that hurt you. I'm going to kill him!" Mom knew I meant it. She started crying and began pleading with me. "Butch, please don't do this. Son, please don't do this. I'm begging you, don't do this. Your life will be forever changed if you do this son. Butch, put down the knife. Butch, please drop the knife. I'm begging you." I dropped the knife and ran to her. We hugged and cried for what seemed like an eternity. A few days went by, and I pretended to be okay and no longer angry. I thought I was pulling a fast one on Mom, but a Mother knows her child.

"Butch, can you come here for a second to help me with something?" "Sure Mom," I replied. She said, "I need your help packing my suitcase, and when you finish, I need you to pack your bag. We're going on a trip to Montgomery, Alabama." I remember thinking, "We must be going to visit Granddad William," whom I'd never met, and other relatives for Thanksgiving. I excitedly packed my suitcase. Mom called a cab, and we rode to the Greyhound bus station. About halfway on the bus ride to Montgomery, I had a sinking feeling in the pit of my stomach. I asked Mom why were we going to Montgomery, and she said, "Butch, we're going there to live." My

76

heart sank. I cried the rest of the way of the trip. We had left everything behind. All the furniture, the television, friends, my girlfriend, everything. All we had were the clothes on our back and what was in our two or three suitcases.

As the bus drove down Dexter Avenue in Montgomery, there was a building on fire. Years later, I was told it was a black radio station that had been firebombed. As I watched the fire, I remember thinking, "Welcome to Montgomery, Alabama, Butch!" Over and over, I said to myself, "I hate this place. I want to go home. I want to go back to Little Rock." I felt like Dorothy in the Wizard of OZ wishing my way back home.

Mom and I moved in with my Grandmother Daisy Anderson Moore whom Granddad William had married some years after Grandmother Flossie died. They had one daughter (my Aunt Regina) who was married. As it turned out, Granddad passed away on November 23, 1969. I don't doubt this was also one of the reasons for Mom's and my fast exit out of Little Rock. I don't remember going to Granddad's funeral or know if Mom got to see him before he died. I never got to meet my maternal Granddad whom I later learned was one of the most respected Black educator's in Alabama.

Grandma Daisy welcomed us into her home with open arms. Mom and I had to have been something else for her to take on, considering she had just lost her husband. Looking back, Grandma was grieving and taking in a single Mom who had recently been victimized and also grieving over the loss of her father, and her angry, "out for revenge," grandson who hated having to leave Little Rock. Goodness knows Grandma was a Saint for taking us in under such circumstances. She turned out to be the soothing balm I sorely needed at that point in my life.

Pictured from left to right are Grandmother Nannie Belle Simmons, Mom, Dad, Aunt Regina Moore James, Grandfather William Moore, and Grandmother Daisy Anderson Moore

Chapter 12

Adjusting to Montgomery

Grandma made our transition to Montgomery as smooth as she possibly could. When we would meet relatives or her friends, she would proudly introduce us and say, "This is my daughter Jean and my Grandson, Butch." Never were the introductions prefaced with, "My Step..." this or that. It was evident from the start; family was important to her. Grandma was attractive, humble, kind, gracious and without question, the best-dressed woman I had ever seen. She went to church every Sunday, and I never heard her swear or saw her smoke or drink. My Grandmother was a retired teacher who had instructed students alongside Granddad in the various school systems he worked. Her favorite pastime was working in the yard, planting flowers and gardening.

I recall one beautiful day when my Grandma was in the front yard planting daisies. "Daisies for a Daisy," I remember thinking to myself. I was about to go play basketball when Mom stopped me and said, "Butch, before you leave, be sure you help your Grandmother." I went outside, with my b-ball in tow and asked Grandma if I could help her. She allowed me to do so. I knelt down beside her, and before she knew it, I had made such a mess of things, she politely said, "Butch, I think I've got it now. You've been a big help. You can go ahead and play basketball." There are two types of help, I guess. One you need and one you don't. The poor woman probably did cartwheels when I left.

Grandma Daisy lived in Sheridan Heights, a sprawling community filled with middle-class families. It was a "black suburb" made up of two sections. The original homes were referred to as the "Old Section," and the newer homes were called the "New Section." Resurrection Catholic Church and its adjacent Elementary School sat in-between the two sections. Behind Resurrection were two basketball courts dubbed "The Goal," a tennis court and a baseball field. Grandma lived in the "Old Section" in Vandy Court; a cul-de-sac referred to as "The Circle." Terrific neighbors surrounded her. The Lewis' resided on the corner of Vandy Drive. The McCalls, Robinsons, Jacksons, Porsches, Halls, Watsons and Moores, no relation, lived in "The Circle." The husbands of the latter three families were retired military. Around the corner and just up the street on Vandy Drive were Grandma's friends, the Herndon family.

Neighbors in "The Circle" were and remain very close-knit. It seemed, when any of the kids were getting into trouble, or contemplating such, one or more of the adults knew beforehand or shortly afterward. It was as if they had communal ESP. Thus, you could find yourself getting a tongue lashing from almost any of the adults if you were misbehaving. Once, I was talking to a girl in front of the Lewis' house when I heard Mrs. Hall (Addie Mae) yell from her porch, "Butch! Who's that girl you're talking to? Do, I know her?" Now, from where I was standing, it was impossible for Mrs. Hall to have seen me unless she had X-ray vision and could see through the Lewis' house. No doubt, someone in "The Circle" had relayed to her I was with the girl. That was typical of the parents in "The Circle." They had the kids' backs and wanted to make sure none of us strayed too far off course. These "watchful and caring eyes" are something fellow neighbor Ricky Watson and I still talk about and appreciate to this day.

It didn't take very long for Mom to find a job after we moved. She was hired as Secretary to the Vice President for Student Affairs at Alabama State University (ASU). I couldn't believe it when I learned my Dad also worked at ASU. What were the odds of my parents ending up in the same city and working for the same employer after not having seen one another in ten years? In the words of William Cowper's lyrics, "God moves in a mysterious way. His wonders to perform." Dad was Chairperson of the Department of Music and Professor of Choral/Vocal Music. I found it interesting neither of my parents had remarried. I wondered if there were a chance they would remarry. That was something I had long hoped for. In any event, at long last, I was finally going to meet my Dad.

Shortly after our move, I met my Aunt Regina, who was every bit as gorgeous as her graduation picture hanging on the wall in the living room, and her husband Titus (Gate) James. The two were made for each other. Uncle Titus hit it off immediately with Mom and me. He stood about 6' 3," was personable, dapper and a former high school and college basketball star. His family consisted of he, his Mom (Ella

Mae) whom everyone called Ms. James and his seven siblings: Amy, Willie Lee (Toot), Catherine (Cat), the twins Neremiah and Jeremiah, Sidney (Cut-Rate), and Rosa (Sister). The entire family embraced my Mother, and I and referred to us as their "cousins." The James clan was widely respected in Montgomery for their closeness as a family and the boys' basketball prowess. After their high school careers ended, each of the sons ultimately received a scholarship to play college basketball. Toot was a former High School All-American.

Being around the James family exposed me to their alma maters, Booker T. Washington Junior, and Senior High schools. The "feeder" relationship of one school to the other was reminiscent, to me, of the former connection between Dunbar and Horace Mann. Convinced, I would be comfortable at Booker T. Junior High; I begged Grandma and Mom to allow me to go there. They agreed, and I started attending the school shortly afterward. Grandma arranged for Mrs. Herndon to take me to school every day.

There's something about "the new kid on the block" that makes some young boys want to try and intimidate the "newbie" or physically take them on. At least that's what happened to me. There was this one kid at Booker T., who lived in Sheridan Heights, that persisted in picking on me at school. This badgering went on for several days. One day, while at my locker, the kid told me he was going to beat me up if I didn't give him my lunch money. Well, I had grown tired of him by now, and I sure wasn't about to give him my lunch money. So, we went ahead and fought, and I gave him a good butt whipping. After the fight had been broken up, he and I were taken to the Principal's office. There, the Principal told me I might be expelled. How the heck could that happen? I hadn't been attending the school a week for crying out loud, and now I faced expulsion. I had never been in any trouble in school before, and I was frightened about the prospect of being thrown out of school.

The next day, I pretended to go to school. I walked out the front door as if I was headed to Mrs. Herndon's house. When I knew, I was out of Grandma's eyesight; I hid behind some bushes up the street. I waited until she left the house so I could return. I went back to the house, climbed into the attic and stayed there all day. The prickly fiberglass, used to insulate the home, made me itch and sneeze throughout. I was terrified of going back to school. First, I feared the guy I fought would confront me with some of his friends, and they'd gang up on me, and second, I was afraid the Principal was going to kick me out of school.

I knew what time my Grandmother would return home, so I climbed down out of the attic before she arrived. When she asked me how my day at school went, I lied and told her everything had gone well. Just as I spoke the lie, a piece of pink fiberglass from the attic fell onto the floor. Grandma knew I was lying. She mumbled, "Um huh." Then said, "I'll let Jean deal with you when she gets home." Those were words I did not want to hear. When Mom came home, I walked up the hall, and Grandma was right behind me. When Mom asked me, "How was your day at school?" I turned and looked at

Grandma who had this, "You better not lie" look on her face. Then Mom said something like, "Be careful what you tell me." I did not know the Principal had called Mom. All I knew was, I had two upset black women glaring at me, one in front, the other behind, daring me to tell a lie. Now, my fear of possibly going up against a gang of boys at Booker T. paled in comparison to what these women might do to me. I told the truth. Grandma must have been clairvoyant because Mom did "deal with me" indeed! She closed the door to my room and laid one good belt whipping on me. No way was I going to try to run out the room because I knew Grandma was standing right outside the door.

I didn't get expelled, but I sure didn't want to go back to Booker T., so I convinced Grandma and Mom to send me to another school. I was enrolled in Cloverdale Junior High School. Once again, Mrs. Herndon was kind enough to drive me to school every day. Talk about a culture shock regarding going to Cloverdale! It was the first time I had ever attended a white school and been around that many white folks. I hated the situation I was in, at first, and felt very uneasy at the school. I believe Sullivan Walker, a ninth grader and football star, and I was the only blacks at the school.

I'll never forget the day, in Mr. Griswold's class, when he handed me my test paper with his grade on it. As the only black kid in the class, all eyes were on me as the students waited to hear Mr. Griswold, whose class was regarded as "hard to pass," call out my grade. Impatient to hear my result, students started asking, "What did he make? What did he make?" Mr. Griswold said, "D!" The classroom erupted in laughter. I had never been so humiliated in my life. Here I was an A/B student in Little Rock and now this. "Surely, these white kids think I'm dumb and incapable of learning," I thought to myself. I sat at my desk, holding back the tears. I wanted to scream and run out of the room.

When I got home, I couldn't stop crying. I remember saying to Grandma, "This would never have happened to me in Little Rock. I hate Montgomery. I want to go home." Grandma put her arms around me and said, "Butch. Don't worry. You **are** at home. Now wipe your tears. I've got something to tell you." She went on to enlighten me about my Granddad William Dewitt Moore and herself, and the key role they had played in educating rural blacks in Alabama. She made me aware Granddad had a Master's Degree in Education. I learned after she had passed away at the age of 100, she did as well. Grandma spoke to me about the Moore family's legacy of academic excellence and discussed Mom and Dad's scholarly achievements. She took the feeling of despair and emptiness running inside of me that day and filled it full with inspiration, hope, determination and the will to succeed. She was planting a "seed" for me to grasp and hold close. From that day forth, Grandma would double and sometimes triple check my Cloverdale homework. We would also play the "dictionary game," where she would give me a word, and I would have to enunciate it, spell it out aloud, then quickly look it up, to see if I was correct and read the meaning to her. One day, while playing the "game," Grandma said from the kitchen, "Loquacious." I thought about how the word sounded, broke it up into syllables, spelled it back to her and looked it up in the dictionary. I was excited to find out I had gotten it right. She said, "Now what does it mean?" I read back, "tending to talk a great deal; talkative." The next thing I heard was my Grandmother pounding the stove and laughing. I realized she had purposely made me look up that particular word because it described my incessant chatter. Boy, we had a good laugh about that! Without question, Grandma gave me back the confidence I needed to tackle my new environment at Cloverdale.

As Mr. Griswold passed out the grades from the next text, the anticipation of the students was even higher than before. Looking back, I don't doubt there had been a wager amongst them that I would get another D or flunk the test. Mr. Griswold handed me my grade, smiled and said, "A." The class was shocked! I could hear some of them say, "I told you so." It was apparent to me, this big, smart kid named Marvin Trott, a star football player who sat behind me, was elated for me. Marvin ended up befriending me and unbeknownst to him, became my first white friend. With Marvin having my back at school, none of the kids were going to mess with me.

One of the strangest things that happened to me at Cloverdale occurred one day in the gym. I noticed there were a lot of guys crowded in the weight room watching something. As I worked my way through the crowd, I heard some guy say, "Look at that. That's amazing. Look at how his body glistens." I moved closer and realized the guys were watching and talking about Sullivan Walker, aka "Butterball" as he was lifting weights. Butterball was the football team's superstar and the strongest kid in school. The white guys were astonished that day by his strength and fascinated with how his body glistened as he sweat. It was a very strange feeling for me. It was as if they were slave owners watching and waiting to buy a "Buck" at an auction. I was pissed off. Several guys realized I overheard them and begged me not to tell Butterball for fear of reprisal. They had reason to be afraid. I made a deal with them that I would keep my mouth shut just as long as they made sure nobody at school messed with me. They agreed. Thirteen years old and I was already honing my negotiating skills.

Something else interesting happened to me which I feel helped me "break the ice" with my peers at Cloverdale. One day in PE class, I was playing a game of five on five basketball with some fellow students. They were fascinated with my dribbling ability and playing style. The PE Coach, who was the eighth-grade basketball Coach, called me over and told me I had just finished playing against some of the starters on his team. On the spot, he asked me to join the squad. I jumped at the opportunity and joined the team. There weren't many games left in the season, so I figured I wouldn't get to play much. Before the season ended, however, I became a starter. Joining the squad enabled me to meet and befriend more kids which led to my becoming more accepted at the school. Although I had a rocky start at the outset, I came to enjoy my time at Cloverdale.

The next year, I attended Goodwyn Junior High, the school in which Sheridan Heights students were recently zoned. Goodwyn would be my fourth Junior High School in three years. Although I didn't realize it at the time, being in different school settings, for such a short amount of time, helped my "adjustment and flexibility" skills. Goodwyn was the largest Junior High School in the nation that year with about 3,000 students. It turned out to be a good fit for me. The school was vibrant and had a lot of student activities. I immersed myself in Goodwyn and came to have nearly as many white friends as I did black. I continued to make solid A's and B's in school and was well-liked for my wit, humor and basketball ability. I was also beginning to grow quite fond of the ladies, and I wasn't bashful about letting them know it. There were some white cheerleaders I liked and am pretty sure liked me back, but it was taboo to fool around with a white girl in Alabama. A black man could be killed for such, so I kept my friendships but didn't cross the line. I stuck with chasing the bountiful crop of black girls in the school.

Admittedly, I was clumsy with females. I didn't have a smooth line, and I tended to act silly around them. I had a reason, though. I was a 14 going on 15-year old adolescent male, whose testosterone was on quadruple steroids, who was looking in the mirror every day to see if I was growing facial hair. Plus, I was having wet dreams at night and wondering how in the hell could that happen and a pimply faced dude for crying out loud! Did I seriously want to date a girl? Nope! Did I want to have sex with a girl? Yep!! And girls knew my intentions.

How could they not? I was too obvious about it. For instance, one day I had the nerve to walk up to a black girl at school and tell her I wanted a ride on the hay wagon. After she had slapped me to the moon and back, and my ears stopped ringing, I realized some things were best left unsaid to a girl. Suffice it to say; I didn't have a girlfriend at Goodwyn.

I tried to convince myself I didn't need girls anyway because by now I was madly in love with basketball. It had become my outlet for releasing my pent-up frustration about that fateful night in Little Rock. I loved the attention I received from playing b-ball, and in kind, I loved the game back by playing as hard as I could. My style of game was "flashy," and I played to the crowd. The more they wanted, the more I would try to give them. I was fast becoming that mesmerizing Philander Smith guard I saw a few years back, and I loved every minute of it.

Wiley Steen was Goodwyn's Varsity Basketball Head Coach. I loved playing for the man because he would let me be myself on the court. Once, at the end of a game, I did Curly Neal's (of the Harlem Globetrotters) one hand on the floor while dribbling in a circle routine, and Coach angrily called a timeout. Instead of chewing me out for "hot dogging," he said, after a long pause, something like, "I love it!" He, I, and the team broke into laughter. Then, Coach sternly said, "Butch, don't ever do that in a game again if I'm your Coach. We do not show up our opponents!" I got the message and never did the routine again.

We had four black players on the team. They were, Anthony Sharpe, whose nickname was "Red" because of his light complexion, Eugene Mays, Larry Ware or "Tater Head" as we called him, and me. Coach Steen was a good man with a big heart. Whenever Anthony and I needed a ride home after practice, he'd give us a lift, paying for the gas out of his pocket, if he wasn't taking Eugene and Tater Head to their homes. I'll never forget him for his generosity.

Goodwyn Junior High Varsity. I'm on the bottom right

Many nights after practice, Red and I had to walk 5.4 miles (that's not a typo[1]) back to Sheridan Heights. We tried not to think too much about it, but it was always a scary situation. On freezing nights, we would stop and go inside a Baskin-Robbins ice cream shop to get warm. Despite the cold temperature outside, we would always

---

[1] Anthony "Red" Sharpe validated the distance on 1/20/2017.

buy some ice cream. I got hooked on pralines and cream, which I still enjoy to this day. Every night, we'd try to thumb a ride home but mostly to no avail. We had to "hump it" all the way home unless someone black stopped to pick us up. There was no way a white person in Montgomery was going to give two black guys a ride after dark.

The scary part of our walk/run home came when we were about a half mile from Sheridan Heights. We had to go through the Chisolm community which, back then, was widely regarded by blacks as the most racist neighborhood in Montgomery. To let blacks know they weren't wanted or welcome in Chisolm, KKK was painted on the pavement on the main street in bold white letters in the middle of the road. When we reached the outskirts of Chisolm, Red and I would make sure we had our books and practice gear close to our bodies. We knew if someone came after us, to not get separated. We'd look at each other and say, "You ready?" We'd answer each other with, "Ready!" Then we'd break into a full speed run and go down a side street. We wouldn't stop until we got to the railroad tracks near Brockway Glass' manufacturing facility, which was well lit. We'd catch our breath, laugh and say, "Made it, again." People in the neighborhood thought we were crazy for taking such a huge risk. We would never have done it if there had been another way home.

Lacking in team height, we won about half our games that year. There were two contests that season which stand out in my mind. The first was our opening game. We played Booker T. Washington Junior

High, and they had a point guard named Willie Frank Perry. Willie Frank lit me up for about 32 points. I had never played against anyone who had dominated me so thoroughly. The second memorable contest was a home game. As I was dribbling up the court, our student section stood up and started going bonkers. They did this several times during the first half of the game. I couldn't figure out what in the world was going on. During a timeout, I asked my teammates what was causing the students to go so crazy. One of them said, "Your skip dribble." "My skip dribble? What are you talking about?", I asked. The teammate replied, "That thing you do when you start hopping and jumping with the ball as you come up the court." I said, "That! That's what they're cheering about?" Several guys chimed in with, "Yep." Still disbelieving, I took a pass from out of bounds and deliberately skipped up the court with the ball. The student section went nuts. I couldn't believe it. My skipping was done strictly for three reasons. First, to help me see what defense the opposing team was playing. Second, to figure out if my defender was trying to make me go left or right. Third, to set up my defender for a crossover dribble so I could leave him in the dust. Never was my so-called "skip dribble" intended for entertainment. I did start doing it intentionally, now and then, just to get the crowd into a game. At the end of the season, Red made First Team All-City, and I was on the Third Team. Years later, Red told me he thought I should have been named First Team. Personally, I would have to give that nod to Willie Frank who was named First Team All-City.

After basketball season, the school's Wrestling Coach came to me with an unusual request. He wanted me to join the wrestling team for the Region Finals. One of his top wrestlers, who was highly ranked in the state, had been kicked off the team by his Dad for poor grades. I thought Coach was out of his mind, considering I had never wrestled competitively before. He had seen me grappling in PE class so; he felt I was an adequate replacement. I agreed to join the team. Coach had one of my friends, Beb White, who was an All-State wrestler, spend several days showing me various moves.

As I stepped onto the mat for my Region match, I experienced butterflies in my stomach again. Coach had failed to tell me I was going up against the Number 1 wrestler in the State in our weight class. He also neglected to share; the kid had won the state championship the past year. Going into the third and final round of the match, I needed to pin my opponent to win. I used Beb's favorite move and dropped my foe onto his back. I wrapped my right arm around one of his legs to give me leverage over him. I had both of his shoulders clearly on the mat for what seemed the requisite two seconds to win the match. Just as the referee's hand hit the mat for the count of two, time expired. It was a bang, bang moment. Goodwyn fans and I thought I had one. The official went to the scorer's table and ruled time had expired before my pin. Our Coach was furious. Some of our fans were so outraged they stormed the floor to protest the call. I never been to a wrestling match before and didn't know fans could get so worked up over a wrestling event.

After the floor had been cleared, the referee signaled for me and my opponent to return to the center of the mat. After a moment or two, he raised the other kid's hand as the winner. Although I was disappointed, I was relieved the match was over. I was completely exhausted and thought to myself, "Man, this wrestling stuff is hard. I won't be doing this again." At the school's sports award banquet, later that year, I received my Varsity basketball letter. When the wrestlers were called up to get their letters, I applauded roundly for them. Then, out of the clear blue, the Wrestling Coach called me up to the podium to receive a Varsity letter. I thought he was joking and didn't leave my seat. The wrestlers convinced me Coach wasn't joking, so I joined him at the podium and received my second Varsity letter on the night. I had earned the wrestling team's respect for taking my opponent, who won the State title again that year, to the final second of my match which they and I thought I had won.

YOU GOTTA PUT IN THE WORK

When I was growing up, there were two things about Mom that were very clear. She was a perfectionist and a hard worker. When she took on something, it had to be done right, or she would do it all over again. This attribute, or "seed," rubbed off on me in a big way. Going into the summer of 1971, I realized I was getting by in basketball primarily on my athleticism. My shot was okay, but not fundamentally sound enough for the high school level, I felt. I also needed to get quicker and become more knowledgeable about the game. So, I set out to improve my shot, my quickness, and become more of a student of the game. Setting goals and following through on them would prove beneficial to me later in life, as I came to learn.

My neighbor, Ricky Watson and I became close friends. Part of what cemented our relationship was our mutual love for basketball. As a result, we played b-ball 2 to 3 times daily at the "The Goal," only stopping to eat lunch or rest for about an hour. Ricky was a staunch defender who made me work hard to get my shot off every time I played against him. I knew if I tweaked my jump shot during the summer, and could get it off on Ricky, I would be able to handle high school defenders. The two of us were mainstays at "The Goal" which was like a basketball "Mecca" in that it drew top players from around the city to it. Games were intense, and there was a lot of pushing and shoving, trash talking and cussing, elbowing and of course the occasional fight. It was ghetto ball in the black 'burbs for sure. Typically, younger guys were relegated, by the older guys, to play on the "Little Court" which was also a full court with two baskets. Older and better players played on "The Big Court," and that's where Ricky and I competed with and against one another.

To further enhance my skills, improve my quickness, and become more knowledgeable about the game, I turned to my cousins the James'. I wouldn't bother to go straight to their house; I would head straight to Booker T.'s gym because I knew that's where they would be. Whenever I played against my cousins, I got taken to "school." Their skills and work ethic were second to none. Every time I thought I knew something about basketball, they would teach me something I didn't know, especially Jeremiah. He was several years older than me and made First Team All-City at Jefferson Davis High after Booker T. had closed. He would go on to play for Abilene Christian College and be named Honorable Mention All-Conference two years in a row. At 5' 7", Jake was that Philander Smith guard reincarnated. He was fast, quick, strong, could jump, shoot, dribble, and was a tenacious defender.

The first lesson Jake taught me was not to reach for the basketball when defending him. One day, while playing a whole court game, I was guarding Jake, and he said, "Don't reach on me. Never reach on me. If you reach, you'll pay!" Inevitably, I learned the hard way. I went for a steal on him, and he hit me so hard with an elbow, it stood me straight up from my bent defensive position. I saw stars, as he said with an assassin's grin, "I told you not to reach on me!" Jake took me under his wings and was like a "big brother" to me. One day, I asked him, "What makes you guys so good? All of you James boys can play." For the next couple of hours, Jake gave me a Ph.D. lesson in b-ball by showing me his workout regimen. Here's some of what he taught me:

BASKETBALL 101

- Steal a b-ball after it leaves a defender's hand and is on the way down to the floor. This type of steal attempt gives you a second chance to get the ball on its way up.

- Do wrist curls, full curls, toe raises, and squats with barbells half your body weight as a beginner, then increase the weight amount as you get stronger

- Do chair jumps over folding chairs, with the back of the chair facing you, to improve your explosion when jumping. (Note: I found out the hard way if you miss jumping over the seat of the chair the back of it will come forward and hit you in the back like a slap. Today this type of drill is called Plyometrics. The James boys were doing this exercise in the mid-60s to early 1970s before the Russians popularized it in the 1970s Olympics. I've always contended the James' were 5 to 7 years ahead of anyone else regarding basketball.

- Do wall squats to strengthen the quads. Place your back against a wall and sit like you're in a chair and hold the position for a minute or longer.

- Stretch daily.

- Do fingertip pushups. This exercise helps strengthen the wrists and fingers which are susceptible to sprains in basketball.

Cognizant I needed to work on improving my shot; I turned to Uncle Gate for advice. He watched me shoot and noticed my right elbow was outward, versus perpendicular to the floor. He demonstrated what he meant and said, "Remember always shoot through the "V." Confident I understood what he recommended, I went up to "The Goal" the next day and practiced for over an hour working on shooting through the "V." I kept trying to look through the slight "V" that was created between my right thumb and index finger when I held the ball above eye level to shoot. This positioning made it impossible to see the basket well. I wondered how it could be possible to see the basket with only a half inch of space to look through. Unable to clearly see the basket, I became frustrated and nearly gave up on Uncle Gate's advice. Finally, I put the ball over my head and just happened to point my elbow toward the ground. When I did, my arms formed a "V," and I could clearly see the basket. I said to myself, "This is what he was talking about!" A shooter was born that day.

The last thing I did was pray for quickness. Although I was relatively speedy, I knew that at 5' 6", I needed to get much quicker for high school basketball. More swiftness, particularly side-to-side, would increase my ability to evade, harass and keep my opponents off balance. Plus, enhanced quickness would make my foe more vulnerable on offense and defense. The next day, during a whole court pickup game, on three consecutive trips down the court, I had faked guys and overrun the ball, thus leaving it behind me. I couldn't figure out what was going on. Then it hit me like a ton of bricks. I was suddenly a step or two quicker than I'd ever been. I looked skyward and said, "Thank you, Lord." Now, I had the burst I needed!

I was a flashy and scrappy player with a short fuse. I loved dribbling between my legs, behind my back and making tricky no-look passes. Ricky once described me as a guy that played with a "chip on his shoulder." Well, I had one indeed. I was small in stature and felt I had a lot of ground to make up considering I had started playing basketball so late in life. It was as if there was a clock ticking in my head to get superb at the game fast because if I didn't, time was going to run out. I was like a small stick of dynamite ready to explode.

Incredibly, I never got into a fight involving basketball at "The Goal" or anyplace else for that matter. I certainly came close several times though and broke up more than a few of them. Somehow, I managed to be the type of mediator that didn't get into a spillover fight with one of the combatants for breaking up the fight. I guess this was a "peacekeeping seed" Mom instilled in me. I did get into a very heated pushing and shoving match once that had a follow-up I'll never forget. I had played several games of one on one at "The Goal" against a kid from "The New Section" who happened to be a member of a local gang. The guy knew he couldn't outplay me, so he compensated by fouling me a lot, and fouling me hard! I got so mad with his constant fouling; I took out my frustration on him by holding him scoreless in several games. The guy went home, and I thought that was the end of things.

That night, as Ricky and I were walking home from a party, four gang members came strolling up the sidewalk. It was the kid from "The Goal" that day, his brother and two fellow gang members, all of whom we knew. The unspoken rule was, when that gang was on the sidewalk, you got out of there way, and off the walkway, to allow them to pass. This night, the group wouldn't let me and Ricky get away with just stepping aside. The members insisted the kid, and I fight. Well aware one of the gang members was proficient with a switchblade; I had no other choice than to fight the guy from "The Goal" that day. I quickly grabbed him, spun him around and threw him into some hedge bushes. I said, "Hit it!" to Ricky, meaning run for your life! For some strange reason, Ricky took what I thought was a long route home and ran around the next block. I took a shorter route by grabbing and jumping the six-foot left field fence of the baseball field. Next, I sprinted across the field and jumped the right field fence near "The Goal." Thinking Ricky was nearby, I yelled, "Come on, Come on." I heard a panting out in the street, and it was him. After catching our breath, we finished our run home.

Two weeks passed, and I didn't go to "The Goal" for fear of the gang's payback. After repeated attempts, Ricky finally convinced me to go up to the basketball courts with him. Not long after we arrived, sure enough, up came the kid's brother. I told him, I didn't want to fight him. He said there wouldn't be one. He went on to inform me his brother confessed he had lied and said I'd beaten him up that day. I asked the brother, "What did you and the gang do?" He replied, "We kicked his a#$!" I asked the brother if I was okay with the crew and he assured me I was. Whew, talk about being relieved.

GUY TRIES TO SHOOT ME

The most frightening thing to ever happen to me was when a guy tried to shoot me at "The Goal." I was playing in a full court pickup game against some guys from across town. They had this 6'3" dude who was outplaying me, had blocked two of my shots, and was talking plenty of trash. Young bystanders were stunned to see me getting whipped. I was having a hard time figuring out my opponent's strengths and weaknesses that day. I finally realized the guy would jump in the air every time I looked like I was going to shoot. Also, he kept guessing wrong when trying to steal the ball from me. Now, I had him figured out and said to myself, "Time to go to work. Nobody is coming from across town and is going to beat us on our court. It's time to take this cat to school! Game's Over!"

I came down the court and gave the guy a pump fake on a shot, knowing he was going to jump and go for the block. He went up in the air, and I caught him on the way down. At this point, I'm talking trash. I said, "Rule number 1. Never, ever leave your feet on me!" He laughed. Later, I came down the court and made a cross-over dribble move on him. He reached for the ball, I pulled back and said, "Rule number 2. (ala Jake) Never, reach for the ball on me!" He laughed. The kids on the sideline were saying back and forth, "Butch is getting ready to school this guy." On one possession, I faked a cross-over move, then dribbled the ball high and outside of my right leg. My adversary reached to try to make a steal. I did a quick cross-over to my left, threw my right elbow hard at him and exploded to the basket for a score. I ran back down the court and felt a hot pain in my elbow. I looked down and saw blood dripping on the court. I glanced at my elbow, and there was a white object sticking out. I was like, "Man, I can't believe this. I hit the guy so hard I broke my elbow." I figured when I touched the white protrusion I would probably pass out from shock. I grabbed the object with my left thumb and forefinger, and it came out. I couldn't believe I hadn't fainted. I looked up the court and saw the guy holding his mouth and bleeding profusely. I had hit him so hard; I knocked out his tooth, and it had gotten stuck in my elbow. He's bleeding, I'm bleeding, and now I'm mad as hell.

I went down the court with the ball, made a shake and bake move, pump faked, and the guy jumped in the air. I took my right elbow and swept his feet right out from underneath him. I pretended like I was fouled on the play and fell to the floor. When he hit the asphalt, a bone shot right out of his skin. It freaked everybody out. I yelled, "That was a foul. It's our ball out of bounds!" Calling for a foul was merely a ploy on my part to keep his buddies from trying to fight me. His pals convinced the guy to drive himself to the hospital. I guess they didn't care that much about him after all. I apologized to them for what had happened as their friend drove off.

Next thing we know, here comes the guy driving back very slowly in his car. The kids watching the game said, "Look, Butch, he's back." I replied, "I know. I see him." I told the kids to get up slowly and walk past the tennis courts and go straight home. I sternly said, "Do not run!" I told all the guys on the court, "He's going to accelerate and try to hit me. You guys on my right, run to the school. Other guys run to the tennis court. When I say hit it, everybody run!" The car picked up speed, and I said, "Hit it!" Everyone got clear. My problem was, in trying to ensure everyone else was safe, I hadn't run and was standing on the court all alone.

The car came to a stop, and the driver's side door swung open. The sun hit this shiny silver object which momentarily blinded me. Everything was in slow motion. I don't know much about guns, but I said to myself, "Holy s#$@! That's a silver plated 44 magnum!" I saw my life flash right before my eyes. I turned and ran, and in three steps, I was full speed and flying. When I realized I was running upright; I started running bent over, thinking, "If he gets the shot off, he's going to have to hit me in my butt, not my back." Weak from shock, my opponent tried but was unable to get the shot off.

I ran to Mr. Rudolph's house for help, (he lived behind Grandma on Vandy Drive), but his kids told me he wasn't at home. I told them a guy was coming after me with a gun and they needed to get on the floor in their bedrooms. I ran out of their back door, jumped the fence and hid behind Grandma's storage house. I thought, "He'll never find me here!" Suddenly, it hit me like a ton of bricks. If the guy asked anyone if they knew where I was, their likely answer would be "The Goal" or his Grandmother's house. I jumped the part of Grandma's fence near the driveway and ran to the side door. I knocked loudly, but she didn't hear me. So, I ran to the front door and pounded it until Grandma opened the door. She asked me, "Butch, what is going on? Is something wrong?" I grabbed her left arm and guided her to her room. I told her I needed her to lock the door and get under the bed. She said something like, "You've gotten yourself in some trouble, haven't you? Well, you know I'm going to tell Jean about this." I said, "Yes Ma'am." At that moment, dealing with Mom and Grandma would have been a walk in the park compared to a guy wielding a gun.

After I had felt my Grandmother was safe, I had one more thing to do. I had to go outside, in case the guy drove up the cul-de-sac, so I could run to steer him away from Grandma's house. With my exit route mapped out in my head, I waited and waited, but the guy never showed up thank goodness. Words can't begin to describe how embarrassed I was as I pulled my Grandmother out from underneath her bed. Man, did I get a verbal beat down from her and Mom afterward! Now, I feared for my life with them about as much as I had the guy with the gun. If you've never faced two angry black women alone, trust me, you don't want to go there.

Before the summer ended, and high school began, Mom and I moved into a house she had rented in the Brookview subdivision, which was next to Sheridan Heights. My guess is, Mom probably felt we'd overstayed our welcome having lived with Grandma for several years. I'm sure Grandma didn't want to see us leave, and am equally sure they both were comforted in knowing we were near one another. The three-bedroom house was in a cul-de-sac, and one house away from the Liggett's whom Mom and I became very close to. Mr. Liggett (James) and his wife Margaret (Mur) had six children: Caroline, James Jr. (Mush), Jerome (Doc), Crystal (Crys), Chad and Pete. After Ricky had moved away, Doc and I became best friends.

Chapter 13
Robert E. Lee High

Booker T. Washington High had been closed a year or so before I started attending Robert E. Lee High in 1971. Lee benefited immediately from the rich talent pool of arriving black athletes from Trenholm Court and Sheridan Heights. Lee won its fifth state football championship in 1970 with Booker T. transfers Michael Lee Washington, Ralph Stokes and George Pugh playing starring roles on the school's first integrated football team. Each went on to sign and play on the gridiron for the University of Alabama. Washington ended up playing nine years in the NFL as a starting cornerback with the Tampa Bay Bucs.

Lee High, which was renowned for its band, academics, and athletics, was predominately white. It was an amalgamation of students from Booker T. Washington Junior and Senior High, Goodwyn, Capitol Heights and Georgia Washington Junior High Schools. Back then, Montgomery area High Schools were grades 10th through 12th. When I arrived as a 10th grader (i.e. sophomore), there was racial tension in the air at the school. Lee's football team, to put things into perspective, had only been integrated the year before. The only major racial event I recall happening that year was when many black students, myself included, and some white students walked out of the school in protest of the playing of Dixie during half-time of

106

football games. My homeroom English teacher, Mrs. Moore, who was black, begged me not to take part in the walk-out, fearing there would be physical confrontations. Despite her plea, I joined my peers nonetheless. Tensions were high outside the school, but thanks to some black seniors, particularly Student Government Association (SGA) Vice-President Curtis Ziegler, things were kept calm. When asked for his recollection of the events, Mush, who played on the football team, told me after the walk-out, the song was no longer played at half-time that season.

Two teachers that stood out to me my sophomore year were Mrs. Moore and Ms. Marlar, my biology teacher. Both were dedicated and excellent educators. They were firm, yet fair. One of the funniest things that happened to me that school year occurred in Ms. Marlar's class. I had created, in my mind, an academic competition with Vanessa Bibb, a brilliant student, who also lived in Sheridan Heights. Competitive by nature, my goal was to outscore Vanessa on every test. I never told her what I was doing. After each test, I would ask Vanessa her score. Invariably, hers would be a point to several points higher than mine. Her higher scores only fueled my competitive fire and upset me to no end. I made up my mind; she was no longer going to outperform me. In preparation for our next assignment, a timed dissection quiz followed by a written test, I stayed up past midnight most nights studying. Incredibly, Vanessa and I were assigned as lab partners for the quiz. No worries, I thought, I could still achieve a higher individual grade on the written test. Our task was to dissect a bullfrog and use colored pins to name its anatomical parts.

I insisted on doing the dissection, even though Vanessa was better at it. The frog was extremely bloated due to formaldehyde absorption, and when I made my incision, I inhaled so much of the colorless gas; it made me high. So much so, as I tried to place pins on various organs of the frog, I kept sticking them into the wooden table. Vanessa kept asking me if I was okay, and I kept telling her I was fine. Truth be told, I was ripped! When I saw the dead frog jumping up and down on the table, I knew it was time to turn the rest of the project over to Vanessa. She got an A for the two of us on the quiz. She had beaten me once again, but this time I felt good (literally) about it and was happy for her. To this day, I don't remember a single thing that happened the rest of the day in school. For all I know, I may have walked the halls singing James Brown's, "I Feel Good," because I sure did. A few years ago, I shared the story with Vanessa. She laughed herself to tears.

That fall, I made the Junior Varsity basketball team, and in the spring I made the Varsity baseball team. The main thing I remember about that b-ball season was I made the team barefooted. Here's what happened. After the first day or so of tryouts, I went to my locker and found it open. I had accidentally left it unlocked, and someone stole my brand-new basketball shoes. Without a backup pair, the next day I tried out in my socks. Well, socks don't grip on a varnished wood floor. I was slipping and sliding all over the place. So, I took off my socks and continued the tryouts barefooted. For once, I was glad I had sweaty feet. The moisture was just enough to give me traction on the floor. Quite naturally, I had some large blisters afterward, but it was either that or face being cut. Initially, my tryout opponents laughed at me about not having shoes on, but after I had started scoring and stealing balls from them, they were silenced! By the time Mom could buy me a new pair of shoes, I had made the team.

In baseball, during one practice, Coach Lee had me in the starting lineup in right field. I couldn't figure out why because the position warrants having a strong throwing arm and mine was average. I was probably better suited for left field. I looked over at the center fielder, who was fast, and thought, "Well, we both can run, so I guess this does make sense." When I stepped to the plate during batting practice, this white catcher said to me, "Butch, the pitcher throws 90 miles an hour, sometimes faster. I gotta tell you; he's wild. Sometimes I don't even know where the ball is going." I thought the catcher was just using one of my tactics of trying to rattle and intimidate the batter. It turned out; the catcher was telling the truth! The pitcher did throw 90, and sometimes faster, but he had no control. The catcher struggled mightily to corral the pitcher's errant throws. The hurler threw three 90 miles per hour baseballs near my head, and he wasn't doing it on purpose. Once, he yelled, "Watch out!" I'm saying to myself, "I've had enough of this. If this guy hits me, the ball is going to kill me." When the guy did throw a strike, it seemed like it was already in the catcher's mitt as I was swinging. I didn't come close to hitting the ball that day. After practice, I went to Coach Lee and told him I was doing the baseball team a disservice. I confided, "Coach, I can't hit a 90 mile per hour fastball. I have decided the best contribution I can make to the school is to continue focusing on my academics and basketball." Coach Lee said, "Are you sure you don't want to stick this out?" My response was, "Coach, with all due respect, I've never been more sure of something in my life." Coach replied, "Then go win us a state basketball championship."

My three-year basketball career at Lee was so-so. My temper tended to keep me in Head Coach Bernard Boyd's doghouse. I'd gotten pretty heated during one practice my senior year. Afterward, in the locker room, as I tried to open my combination lock, it wouldn't open. I repeatedly tried to open it, but couldn't. My teammates were laughing hysterically, and I was getting madder and madder. It turned out; I had left my locker unlocked, and a teammate had swapped locks with me as a joke. I completely lost it and went into a profanity-laced, locker punching tirade that cost me dearly. Coach Boyd heard and saw my outburst. Following, he did what any good Coach would do. He taught me a lesson by reducing my playing time. My outburst wasn't my first temper tantrum while on the team. I don't know why I was so volatile at that age. Was it my lack of height? Was it because I was fatherless? Was it because I was experiencing the life of a black man? I don't know what it was, but it wasn't how my Mom had raised me.

That senior year, one of my most memorable games came against our crosstown rival Sidney Lanier, at their gym. The contest was played before a standing room only crowd. Early in the battle, we were losing, and I was sitting on the bench. Out of the blue, some of our students starting chanting, "We want Butch! We want Butch!" They repeated the refrain until it spilled over to the Lanier student section and their fans. Virtually the entire gym was chanting, "We want Butch!" Awestruck, I looked at Red and said, "Man, this is crazy!" His response was, "You better get ready because you're about to go in."

Coach put me in, much to the crowd's delight. Within minutes, I blocked a 6' 3" guy's jump shot as he released the ball about 18 feet away from the basket, stole several balls, scored 4 points and hit a half-court shot to beat the buzzer right before halftime. The fans in the gym were going nuts! I don't remember if we won or lost, but several girls were waiting for me in the lobby after the game. I was so busy getting their phone numbers; I nearly missed the team bus back to school.

The most embarrassing thing that ever happened to me on a High School basketball court was when I broke a new jock strap in the middle of a game. I was dribbling down the court on a fast break and exploded off my left leg to go to my right. Suddenly, I heard a loud Pow! I thought surely; I had torn my hamstring. I didn't feel any pain, however, so I continued the play and made a jump shot from the top of the key. As I was running back down the floor, I felt a cool breeze in my groin area. I looked down and saw part of me and part of my jock strap hanging from underneath my basketball shorts. I bent over and quickly tied the broken jock strap piece around the waistband of the jock. I managed to stay in the game without an equipment change, but the accident caused quite a stir in the stands.

Later that season, I helped our squad make it to the state tournament by hitting the winning shot in the regional finals against Opelika High. We were eliminated in the quarterfinals of the state tournament by eventual champion Hayes High. Based on Hayes' margin of victory during the tournament, it could be easily argued we were the number two team in the state that year. Many years later, Mom told me Coach Boyd called her my senior season and told her he was reducing my playing time because he wanted me to learn the importance of being able to control my temper. Mom had agreed with Coach's decision. I was astonished to learn the two were in cahoots together that season. Admittedly, they were both right, and I did learn a valuable lesson that year. I also heard an Auburn recruiter had come to one of our practices and asked Coach who his three best players were. Coach told the scout they were, Wiley Peck, who went on to star at Mississippi State and play in the NBA for the San Antonio Spurs, Jerome Liggett, who would later be inducted into Auburn University at Montgomery's (AUM) Basketball Hall of Fame and Butch Simmons. I said to myself, "Well I'll be damn!" My respect for Coach Boyd only grew with these revelations. A year later, I went to a Lee basketball practice and told Coach my Mom had "spilled the beans" on him. We had a good chuckle about that. I also thanked him for trying to help me get my head on straight.

112

Having taken college preparatory courses throughout High School and possessing a B+ grade point average, I was accepted for admission by each of the colleges to which I had applied. My focus was on attending Grambling State University. I was somewhat familiar with the institution, and the town, due to having spent part of one summer with Mom's close friends, the Morrows (Archibald and Montez), who were Physical Education instructors at the University. Mrs. Morrow, who graduated from Philander Smith with Mom, and her husband had two son's Selwyn and Syrone whom I used to spend the night with back in Little Rock. Coach and Mrs. Morrow were going to let me live with them, thereby defraying my cost for room and board. Factoring in Grambling's solid basketball program, it was a perfect scenario, I felt.

With graduation growing near, I could sense Mom was beginning to feel a sense of loneliness related to my expected departure to Grambling. I decided to meet with my guidance counselor, Mrs. Rowell, to get her thoughts about schools closer to home that I may not have considered during my college search. She smiled as if she knew something I didn't know. Apparently, she had been waiting for quite some time for my inquiry. Proudly, she said, "Have you considered my alma mater Auburn University?" I told her I hadn't but did share how much I enjoyed watching their football team play. I expressed to her I felt Auburn's team was a lot like me, an underdog, and that I loved rooting for underdogs. Mrs. Rowell gave me glowing reviews about the University during our conversation. Shortly afterward, Mom and I drove up to Auburn to tour the school.

When we took the Auburn University exit off I-85, I didn't know what to expect. I had never been to the campus, nor had I seen pictures of it. As the buildings began to appear beyond the trees, the moment became magical. I was so stunned by the beauty of the campus, Mom said, "Butch, close your mouth son." It was love at first sight. Auburn was everything I had imagined how a large University would appear. It was based in a small town with the University being its main focal point. I told Mom, "This is it! This is it! This is where I'm going to go to college."

Days later, I went to Mrs. Rowell's office and shared my excitement about my Auburn visit. She said, "I knew you would like it. I think it's going to be a great fit for you." Following, Mrs. Rowell helped me fill out the necessary application paperwork. I was applying very close to the acceptance deadline, but she felt confident we would beat the target date. Not long after my submission, I received a letter of acceptance to the Institution. When I shared the news with Mrs. Rowell, we hugged and jumped up and down with glee.

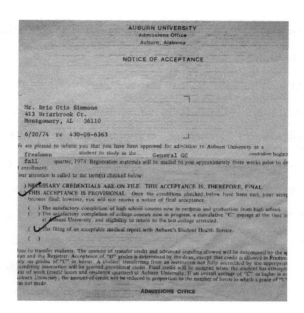

Academically, I ended up graduating from Lee in the top 10 percent of my class of over 600 students. During my three years at the school, there were times, however, when I was anything but a model student. Like when:

- Doc and I snuck a few beers onto the bus before the basketball team rode to Selma High for a game.

- I'd stand at the bottom of the stairs between classes and try to look under girls' dresses as they were ascending the stairs heading to class.

- I was talking to a girl and another young lady, who was built like a Coca-Cola bottle, passed by. My eyes followed her hips all the way down the hall. When I turned around, the girl I had been talking to had vanished.

- After four years of trying, I finally convinced a girl whom I had known since Junior High School, to go out on a date with me. I took her to Lee's homecoming football game, and at halftime, as girls walked around Crampton Bowl, my head was on a swivel as I followed their hips with my eyes. It turned out my date was watching me the whole time as I was surveying the other "eye candy" in the stadium. We never dated again.

- I took Driver's Education three years in a row, on purpose. The class had simulated cars much like bumper cars. Whenever a driving simulation movie would come on, and we were to get on the road and drive, I would make illegal turns, crash into things, speed; you name it. I'm sure I drove Mr. Crippen, and Mr. Mitchell crazy those three years.

All in all, when I wasn't cutting up or flirting, I was a conscientious student, and I had an enjoyable experience at Robert E. Lee.

PREPARING FOR AUBURN TRYOUTS

With my college choice solidified, I mapped out a summer workout plan in anticipation of trying out for Auburn's basketball team. My strategy involved putting myself through the most grueling training I had ever gone through in my life. Daily, I was going to leave home and dribble a basketball in my right hand for 1 mile, then practice my shooting for 4 hours (no less than 500 jump shots per workout session). Next, I would dribble the ball in my left hand for 1 mile on my way back home. I would do 100 pushups and sit-ups each day. I would play 3 to 4 games twice a day against the best competition in the city. I would also run 1 mile for every training regimen I didn't complete. I had reconciled, that while I couldn't control my height, the one and only thing I had complete control over was how hard I worked. I made up my mind that summer, "No One Was Going to Outwork Me!" This mindset would prove beneficial to me later in life. Mom' work ethic "seed" was germinating inside me.

That summer, my blue Chevy Nova was perhaps one of the most recognized cars in Montgomery. I would wake Doc up early each morning and off we'd go to pick up "our boys" on the way to playing basketball games around the city. "Our boys" were Jeffrey Boswell (JB), Ricky Cotton (King C), Michael (Mike) Dudley, "Tweet" our mascot so to speak, and sometimes Wiley (Stretch) Peck. It had to have been a sight to see six to seven guys, ranging in height from 5' 7" to 6' 7," sitting on one another's laps, packed in a small Chevy Nova like sardines. We were unbelievable as a team. JB, who had one of the prettiest jumps shots I'd ever seen, was my height at 5' 7" and like me, he could light it up scoring from outside. He would go on to become a First Team All-City player at Carver High and play collegiately. The ambidextrous 6' 3" Doc was virtually unstoppable. Years later, the Montgomery Advertiser named him the best player, in a 25-year timespan, in the city. Wiley, at 6' 7", was a rebounding and shot blocking machine. He would go on to become an All-SEC performer, lead the league in rebounding, and get drafted in the 1st round by the NBA's San Antonio Spurs. King C was a 6' 2" athlete who went on to play quarterback and wide receiver for Alabama State. Mike stood 6' 4" and was ever so steady with his smooth mid-range left-handed jump shot. After joining the military, he became an All-Air Force basketball player. Everywhere we played, we struck fear into guys. Most games were blowout wins, but if a contest got precariously close, we would just get the ball to Doc and get the hell out of his way. We were so dominating as a team that summer; we didn't lose a single game.

One night, as I was walking home after a neighborhood party, I overheard some guys, who I thought were my friends, laughing and joking about my plan to walk-on at Auburn. I heard them say, "He's crazy if he thinks he's going to walk-on and make Auburn's team. He's too small. He'll never do it." Just goes to show, those who you think are your friends, may not be. Although the remarks hurt and were cutting, I used them as added motivation regarding my dream. I decided to work even harder and longer. I added shooting at night to my workout routine.

I would go up to "The Goal" after dark, and practice shooting jumps shots with my eyes closed. My goal was to train my mind into remembering the distance and location of the basket once my eyes were shut. I called it training my mind's eye. All I had to do was see in my mind's eye the ball going into the basket. I knew I had missed a shot when I didn't hear anything. I knew I had made a shot, or come close to doing so when I would hear the net swish or the rim clang. Over time, I could tell when I made a clean shot into the basket. Sometimes, though, I would cheat and open my eyes at the last second to confirm I had made the shot. Something else that motivated me that summer was when I read in the newspaper Auburn had signed five High School Basketball All-Americans who would be entering school the same time as me. The signings raised the stakes, in my mind, and made me even more determined to make the team.

That summer was the hottest in Montgomery's history. Almost daily, temperatures hovered at or above 100 degrees. I practiced on a court in an undeveloped area behind the "New Section" called "The Bottom." I hated the baskets there because they had double rims, which my eyes never seemed to be able to adjust to, and chain nets. I figured if I could make shots there, I could make them anywhere. Most days when I practiced, it had to have been over 105 degrees on the court. It was so hot on the concrete; the heat singed my hair causing it to turn red. Upon seeing my hair one day, Donald Jackson, one of the kids that lived in "The Circle," started calling me "Baby Red."

One day, a good friend of mine, Walter Long, nicknamed Doughbelly, or just Dough for short, walked the short distance from

119

his house onto the court. He admonished me for practicing in such heat. He said, "Butch, I heard you dribbling and shooting out here. You do know it's over 100 degrees, don't you? It's too hot for basketball. Whatever it is you're doing is crazy. You are killing yourself. Nobody should be out here in this heat. This is nuts!" I looked at Dough and said, "Well, I gotta know. I just gotta know." "Know what?" he asked. I replied, "I gotta know if I am good enough to make Auburn's team. I just gotta know." He responded, "Well since you gotta know something, do you know you need some water and that you're gonna need to stay hydrated if you're going to be out here?" Thank goodness for Doughbelly looking out for me. I never told anyone I was going be practicing alone daily at "The Bottom" in that summer's stifling heat. It never dawned on me to take water with me for my training sessions. I could have easily suffered a heat stroke from dehydration, and no one would have known I was out on the court. Dough and I both laughed at me overlooking taking the necessary precautions. From that day forward, I would take a break or two from my training regimen and go to his house to get hydrated.

Every day, I tried to push myself beyond my mental and physical limits. It was punishing stuff. I believed if my mind were providing me with "the want to," then my body would listen and respond. Whenever I got tired, I would say a verse from my favorite childhood book, "The Engine That Could." I would say to myself, and out loud, "I think I can, I think I can." When I was dead tired, I would say to myself, and out loud, "I know I can, I know I can." I'd rather have died trying that summer than not to have tried at all as relates to my preparation for Auburn's tryouts. I had to know what I was made of, what type of player and man I was and could become. I had hopes and dreams in front of me, and I was not going to be denied. This drive and competitiveness would serve me well, years later, in Corporate America.

Per the NCAA's website, in 2015 the odds of a high school basketball player competing for a Division I team was **1%**. I don't know what my odds were in 1974, but I'm certain as a 5' 7" walk-on back then they were lower than 1%. I was aspiring to do something that was virtually impossible. I knew there were a lot of doubters, and naysayers out there about my chances, but what they didn't know about me was, I loved proving people wrong! I lived for it!

About a month before school was about to start, Auburn's Student Housing Office contacted me to make me aware all the male dorms were full. No rooms being available didn't come as a big surprise to me, considering I had applied so close to the applicant deadline, but now I had to scramble to find one. The football team had already reported to campus, so I reached out to Secdrick McIntyre, a fellow Lee grad, who was starring on the football team and would go on to play in the NFL with the Atlanta Falcons. Sed, or Mac as we called him, suggested I contact Mike McCloud (aka Cloud), whom I had graduated with at Lee. He thought Cloud might be looking for a roommate. I called Cloud and shared my dilemma. He told me he'd love for me to room with him in the two-bedroom apartment if I didn't mind the fact he already had a roommate (Ronald Wright). He felt Ronald wouldn't object to me moving in either. I told Cloud, I'd be willing to make a cot and sleep on the floor if need be. He suggested I sleep on the apartment's fake leather sofa instead. The three of us agreed to split the rent and utilities, and I moved in with my new roomies shortly afterward. The arrangement turned out to be a win-win scenario for all. One of the cool things about my roommates was, like me, they too were aspiring Auburn walk-on athletes. In their case, they were trying out for the football team.

Chapter 14

Auburn University

My first full day on campus, I walked over to the huge netted bird cage where our mascot, War Eagle, was housed. I wanted to see the majestic bird fly, so I started egging him on to come out of his bird house. The next thing I knew, War Eagle flew out of the house and swooped down right at me. He hit the netting and knocked me flat on my butt. That was my first "Welcome to Auburn" moment for sure.

Auburn is referred to as "The Loveliest Village On The Plains." Apparently, the moniker was taken from a line in a poem by Oliver Goldsmith. As a freshman, however, I heard the evolution of "The Loveliest Village ..." came from Playboy magazine's choice of Auburn having the most beautiful women of any college in America. Whether the Playboy story was true or not, I totally agreed with the assertion! The women at Auburn were stunning! In my mind, the school's battle cry of "War Damn Eagle!" didn't have anything to do with our bird of prey mascot. As far as I was concerned, it could have been a male mating call to all the beautiful women who densely populated the University.

Having taken college preparatory courses in high school, I was well prepared for my freshman curriculum at Auburn. My first semester, I took classes like Spanish II, and Calculus II to name a few. As with any college neophyte, I had difficulty finding my way around and locating my classrooms at first. Demographically, the University had over 16,000 students, of which roughly 300 were black. Being less than 2% of the student body, most of the blacks got to know one another over the course of the semester. At the time, Auburn had one black fraternity and sorority, Omega Psi Phi and Delta Sigma Theta.

From my vantage point, there was a feeling-out process going on between blacks and whites at the school. I strongly suspected there were many white students and faculty, that didn't want blacks at "their fine institution of higher learning." I also sensed most of the black students knew we were "trailblazers" at the University, and that we were not only representing ourselves and our families but our race as well. I felt, we knew the place we were in was a microcosm of race relations in the south and that we were duty-bound to succeed and disprove the myths about us as a people.

One circumstance that occurred during homecoming festivities that year did make me feel somewhat uneasy about my new environment. A white fraternity was emboldened enough to have its members ride on horseback while wearing Confederate uniforms and proudly waving Confederate flags. One of the members rode a white horse! I remember thinking, "What the hell!" Mind you; this was the same fraternity that had an oversized Confederate flag hanging on the front of its frat house. I honestly thought a huge fight was going to break out between blacks and members of that fraternity that day.

Fraternity Members on Horseback in 1974

Fortunately, such situations were few and far between, as far as I knew.

MY BASKETBALL TRYOUTS AND OUTCOME

When basketball tryouts were announced, prospective players reported to Memorial Coliseum with the scholarship players. To my amazement, 52 walk-ons showed up! After the walk-ons' player data was gathered; height, weight, high school attended, playing experience, etc., Coaches, scholarship players and walk-ons were led outside. There, the Head Basketball Coach, Bob, informed us we were going to do a 5-mile run. Our route was outlined with orange cones and other markers. Most of the distance was through a wooded area. After we had completed the course, we were given our times and told to return the next day. We didn't play any basketball. The next day, we did the 5-mile run again, received our clockings and still didn't play any basketball. By now, some of my fellow walk-ons were starting to

125

complain. I remember one guy saying, "I thought I was trying out for the basketball team, not the track team!" A few other walk-ons mumbled, "Me too." The third day, about half of the walk-ons, it seemed, didn't show up. I remember thinking, "Man, they're dropping like flies. Thank goodness, I did all that distance dribbling and running this summer." Admittedly, although I was in tip-top shape, I hadn't trained for daily 5-mile runs.

On Day 3, we had another 5-mile run. As we entered the woods, I overheard some of the scholarship players say they were going to take a shortcut through the woods. Taking a shortcut was a risky proposition considering Coaches were interspersed throughout the woods in places where they thought players might try to take a shortcut. When I saw several players leaving the route and cutting through the forest, I followed suit. I figured it was worth the risk because I was sick and tired of the dreaded "5-mile run." When we returned, our times were checked. Coach Bob knew something fishy had happened. So, he led us to the track and field facility. There, every player had to run a timed 400-yard dash, 220-yard dash, and a 100-yard dash. When we finished, I couldn't feel my legs and collapsed on the track. I wasn't alone. After the players had recouped, we went to the auxiliary gym and played three on three basketball. "Basketball Finally!" I remember thinking. After each game, players, intermixed with walk-ons and scholarship players, were assigned new teammates and would rotate to another basket until all teams had played on each basket in the gym.

After each day, there would be a list of names on the bulletin board at the entrance of the Varsity locker room. If your name wasn't on the board, you had been cut. Fortunately, my name continued to stay on the board. One day, I had a terrible outing and was certain I was going to be cut. On my way to the locker room, I was walking next to Team Captain and All-SEC Academic performer Gary Redding, (aka Redbird because of his leaping ability). I said, "Redbird. Man, I blew it! Of all the days for me to have my worst day. I'm going to get cut." Redbird replied with something along the lines of, "Butch, what are you talking about? You're not getting cut. You're the talk of the Coaches. You're on the team." I responded, "Come on man. Stop jerking me around." Gary recommended I go out the next day, relax and just play my game. When we got to the locker room, I looked at the bulletin board, and mine was one of five remaining names.

The next day, I probably had my best showing during the tryouts. I was relaxed and nearly unstoppable. After we had concluded, Coach Bob told the walk-ons he wanted to speak with us in the locker room. When we walked in, there were no names on the bulletin board. What could this mean? Did we all get cut? My heart was in my throat. We sat down on a bench. I was seated farthest from the door. A 6' 7" redheaded kid from Indiana named Mike Wilson, whom the players dubbed "Red," was next to me.

Coach thanked the five of us for our hard work and effort during the tryouts. Next, he said, "The following two individuals will be members of the Auburn University basketball team." The first

127

name he called was, "Butch Simmons." I let out a, "Yes!" I was about to jump in the air when I realized it was not the time to celebrate. Four other walk-ons, who had worked their tail off, just like me, sat anxiously awaiting their fate. Ensuing, Coach said, "Mike Wilson." Red, who was quiet by nature, smiled and perhaps taking my cue, held his emotions in check out of respect for the three walk-ons who didn't make the team. Coach thanked each of them again and encouraged them to try out next year. When they left, Red and I thanked Coach Bob for the opportunity. He told us we had earned it and deserved it. Red and I were hugging and congratulating one another when the scholarship players came in. They congratulated us and welcomed us to the team.

At the end of the day, all my hard work and sacrifice over the summer paid huge dividends. At 5' 7" and 147 pounds, I had walked on at Auburn, beat out 50 guys for one of 2 spots and made the basketball team. I had defied seemingly insurmountable odds and overcome them. The apple hadn't fallen far from the tree.

PRE-SEASON PRACTICE

Before the 1973 season, the NCAA prohibited freshman at Division I schools from playing Varsity football and basketball. Participants played at least one, sometimes two years on their school's Junior Varsity. The ban was lifted in 1973 and freshman became eligible for Varsity competition in the two sports. During the 1974-75 basketball season, the Southeastern Conference had at least three schools, Auburn, Alabama, and Kentucky, that fielded Junior Varsity teams. At Auburn, all 5 of our incoming freshman All-Americans made the Varsity, with two making appearances on the Junior Varsity that season. Red and I were the only freshman walk-ons on the Junior Varsity. There was one other walk-on who was a returning second year player on the unit. The rest of the squad consisted of scholarship sophomores and one scholarship junior.

I learned quickly, the difference between high school and college basketball is like night and day. First, the court is bigger. A high school court is 84' x 50' in dimension. A college court, on the other hand, is 94' x 50'. The game is also much more physical. The players are bigger, faster, stronger and more athletic. In college, the workouts are far more rigorous and intense. In high school, you might have 2 or 3 exceptional players. At the DI level, all the players are talented. I also learned the life of a college athlete isn't nearly as glamorous as it may seem from the outside looking in. The demands are such; it is a full-time job. Add academic study to the mix, and it is a challenging load for a student to take on. Many days, after practice, I would return to the apartment so tired I would have to take a nap before I could begin studying.

My 1974 fall practice season was extremely challenging. Our scrimmages were so physical; we might as well have been playing football without pads. Coach Bob wanted us to be physical and told us he was preparing us for the NBA. Five members of the varsity squad that year would go on to play or be drafted by an NBA team. Another player, who came the following year and then transferred to another school, also got drafted.

When we started practicing as a team, our vertical jumping ability, stamina, and endurance were evaluated. To assess our vertical leaping ability, we did a tip machine drill. It involved jumping as high as you could and grabbing, then pulling down a retractable rim. After each round, the basket would be placed 2 inches higher. Players could take a running start if they needed. If you missed an attempt, you were dropped out of the next round of the drill. At the height of 10' 4," some players started struggling to grab the rim. I mistimed my jump and didn't pull the basket down, but I hit it hard enough to be allowed to move to the next round. At 10' 6," a few players missed the height. I guess the Coaches figured a 5' 7" guy couldn't make the height, so I was told I could pass and sit out the rest of the drill. I had other plans, though. I said to the Coaches I felt I could make the height and wanted to give it a try. Because I had nearly missed the previous elevation, players and an Assistant Coach supervising the drill moaned and groaned about my request. They thought allowing me to take my turn would only drag out finishing the session. Eventually, I was given the opportunity to try the height. I told the Assistant Coach I needed a running start from half-court for my try. My request exasperated the players, and I'm sure they were ready to run me right out of the Coliseum. Once again, the Assistant Coach acquiesced. When I got to half court, I measured off six inches on my right hand by using two of my left fingers, which were exactly one inch in width. For each inch from my right wrist, I pushed a left fingernail into my skin until I got to 6 inches which turned out to be just underneath my fingertips. Because I could easily grab the rim standing still, my rudimentary pre-jump hand measurement further convinced me I could indeed make the height.

After some stretching, I started rocking back and forth like a high jumper, as I focused on the rim. Mentally, I kept seeing myself making the height. I burst down the court and reached my top speed before I jumped, then everything was in slow motion. I grabbed the rim, pulled it down and held it until the yellow indicator light behind the backboard went off. I generated so much force when I pulled the basket down, my legs swung out to near horizontal. I was so excited about my jump; I didn't give my legs a chance to come back to a vertical alignment, and I prematurely let go of the rim. Now, I was falling backward towards the floor headfirst. Everything now was in super-slow motion. Instinctively, I placed my head on both knees and wrapped my arms behind my knees. I relaxed and went limp on my way down to the floor. I knew when I landed on my back; I would have to immediately pop-up off the floor to lessen the impact from hitting the surface. As soon as I hit the floor, I did a backward flip, like I used to do on the trampoline, and landed on both my feet like a gymnast. The Coaches and players were flabbergasted. After I had been checked on and found to be uninjured, the drill resumed. The rim was placed at 10' 8," and some players missed the height. When my turn came, I told the Coaches I wanted to give the height a try. Not a single person complained this time. Everyone seemed to be wondering if I could make the height. I knew I couldn't make it, but I couldn't resist taking liberty with the guys now. I jogged to half court and started rocking back and forth as I'd done previously. The players started swaying in unison with me. I stopped and asked one of the Coaches if I could pass on the attempt. Players and Coaches gave a deep sigh, as I chuckled inside.

We had another drill in which we were timed jumping over orange sawhorses. We had to hop as long and as fast as we could. It was brutal! Many a player hit the top of a sawhorse and fell. After several days, we complained so much about the drill; I guess Coach Bob got the message and finally had us stop doing it. For about a week or so, we also would go to the weight room and lift. We did bench presses, leg curls and squats to name a few. One day, in the auxiliary gym, Coach Bob stopped practice. He had noticed over the past few days; the guards were having a lot of trouble shooting basketballs. He asked us collectively what we thought the problem was. No one spoke up, so I told him our arms were tight from so much weight lifting. The other guards chimed in and agreed. Coach Bob later reduced the amount of lifting the guards had to do.

We also ran all the steps (aka stairs) of the 12,000 seat Memorial Coliseum on a few occasions. I hated running the Coliseum. If going up the stairs wasn't bad enough, going down them was even worse. The gravitational pull would make me go down faster than I wanted, and trying to slow down would strain my thighs mightily. About half way around the Coliseum, I would be ready to drop. Players would try to rest on the rails at the top of the facility when we thought we were beyond the Coaches' eyesight, but that didn't help much. The stairs were every bit as excruciating as the sawhorses.

On any given day, practice might consist of: position specific drills, half court, and full court scrimmages, learning and running our offensive and defensive plays, rebounding and blocking out drills, to name some. After practice, we'd shoot free throws and have free throw shooting contests to see who would have to run additional suicides (a conditioning drill where you run and touch every line on the basketball court). Boy, did we run suicides! So much so, sometimes guys would puke.

HOW I GOT THE NICKNAME FLEA

I've often been asked how I got the nickname "Flea" when I was playing basketball at Auburn. The name came about during a scrimmage one day. I was having an incredible scoring day, and when I had scored about 24 points, one of the Coaches started yelling and screaming at guys saying, "I can't believe you guys can't stop this little Flea. Can someone please stop him? Can anyone stop him?" Throughout the scrimmage, the same Coach kept calling me Flea, and

133

the more he said it, the madder I got. When I scored about my 28th point, the Coach called timeout and chewed players out for not being able to defend me. I walked up to him and said, "Coach my nickname isn't Flea. My nickname is Butch." Well, most of the black guys on the team overheard me disavow being called Flea. That was a no-no on my part. I should have known not to disown a nickname around a bunch of African American brothers because the name will stick. Next thing I know, all the guys started calling me Flea during the scrimmage. From that point on the name stuck. Over time, I grew to like it because it touched on some of my qualities as a player. I was small, quick, could jump, and was a nuisance to opponents. Plus, Coaches, teammates, and fans liked the moniker. To this day, a lot of people I went to Auburn with still call me Flea.

MY FIRST TENNESSEE GAME

Just before the start of the season, my basketball shoes finally arrived. The Coaches apparently hadn't figured a player my size would be on the team and thus didn't order any size 9 1/2 shoes. When I went to the equipment room to pick them up, the equipment manager told me he thought I was the best small point guard that had ever come through Auburn. I said, "I don't know about that. John Mengelt (of the Chicago Bulls) and Eddie Johnson (Auburn's Freshman All-American the year before) aren't too shabby." The manager said, "I mean under 6 feet tall." I thanked him when he handed me my shoes and confidently walked down the hall in total agreement with him.

Our Junior Varsity Coach was Robert (aka Bobby) Pritchett, who was Auburn's first black Coach. He had played high school basketball in Atlanta with future NBA Hall of Famer Walt Frazier (my man) of the New York Knicks. As a collegian, Coach Pritchett had been an All-American at Albany State. He came to Auburn from Price High in Atlanta with his High School All-American and future NBA All-Star, Mike (Tree) Mitchell. Coach Pritchett was a tad bit taller than me, so, we could relate to one another as small basketball players. As a freshman getting acclimated to college basketball, he was the perfect Coach for me. After I had learned about his playing background, I used to challenge him to games of one-on-one after practice. I won most of the time, primarily because I was much younger than he, but there was no doubt he had been an All-American player. He was superb!

Coach Pritchett had me come off the bench as the sixth man during the season. We talked about me starting, but he felt, and I agreed, it was best for the team having me come off the bench. I provided a "spark," and I was playing the same number of minutes as the starter ahead of me, so it was a win-win all the way around. My biggest thrills that year were playing against the University of Tennessee, and the University of Alabama in front of packed houses. It was an amazing experience I will never forget.

Our trip to Knoxville that season was my first Southeastern Conference (SEC) basketball game. The atmosphere in Stokely Center was electric and intense. As we ran onto the court before the game, Vols students threw oranges at us. It was payback for some of our fans having thrown oranges at Tennessee's football players during the contest between the two schools that season. Fortunately, none of us were injured.

Tennessee had a very talented Junior Varsity team consisting of several High School All-Americans. During warm-ups, I knew I was going to have a good game because I'd only missed one shot while getting loose. I found Stokely Center to be a "shooter's gym." indeed. When I got into the game, Tennessee had a white kid who was talking trash non-stop. He asked me if I knew who he was. I didn't say one word. He said, "I'm a High School All-American!" and he kept talking and talking. The whole time he was chatting, I was timing the rhythm of his dribbles. I would count to myself, "1001, 1002, 1003." I was setting "Mr. Diarrhea of the Mouth" up for a steal. I swiped a pass he tried to throw across the court and raced down the floor with the ball. I pulled up about 30 feet from the basket to shoot. Coach Pritchett yelled, "No, no, no, Flea, that's too far!" After the ball had gone through the net, Coach yelled, "Now that's a great shot baby!"

At one point in the game, the High School All-American looked at me and said, "Why don't you talk. Say something. Hey man, I'm talking to you!" Again, I'm counting in my head, "1001, 1002, 1003." Finally, I said, "I've got something to say." He said, "Oh yeah.

What's that?" I said, "I just stole the ball from you." I went down the court and scored on a layup. The All-American didn't say another word the rest of the game.

MY FIRST ALABAMA GAME

When I was growing up in Arkansas, there was only one major university in the state, and that was the University of Arkansas. It seemed natural to me our biggest rival would be the University of Texas, which bordered our state to the southwest and was a fellow member of the Southwest Conference (SWC). When Mom and I moved to Alabama, there were two major universities, Auburn and Alabama. People tended to be for one school or the other. I naturally gravitated towards Auburn. They were the underdog, the "Little Train" that could, just like me.

I would imagine every young athlete in the state of Alabama dreams of playing in an Auburn/Alabama game. I am one of the fortunate ones who can say they played in one. When the two schools compete against one another, the atmosphere is electrifying and quite like no other for players and fans. That basketball season, I had looked forward, with much anticipation, to playing against our arch rival. When the time finally arrived, my adrenaline level was through the roof! When my teammates and I walked out of the visitor's locker room and headed out onto the floor of Coleman Coliseum for our pre-game warm-ups, the cavernous arena was virtually empty. When the doors were opened to let students in, there was absolute pandemonium. Students were pushing and shoving, knocking down one another and jumping over chairs trying to get the best seats available so they could watch, up close, the state's two biggest schools play against one another. It was a site to see. Right before tipoff, the 11,000-seat arena was filled-to-capacity.

As we were warming up, I looked at my teammate Emmett (Timmy T) Thomas and said, "Timmy T, check this out. Do you see that? Their guys aren't even looking at us. They won't make eye contact. It's like they think they're better than us and they've already won the game." Emmett looked down the court and said, "Yeah Flea, I see what you mean." I said, "Let's go kick their pompous a#$!" The significance of the game was such; both teams deployed one or more of its Varsity High School All-Americans. With one of our Varsity Freshman High School All-American guards joining our squad, I automatically assumed my minutes would be reduced during the game. That did not happen, though. Our new teammate was having difficulty guarding Alabama's freshman point guard who was an All-State player from Bibb County High and who had broken the state High School scoring record the year before. Six minutes into the game, Coach Pritchett put me in and didn't take me out the rest of the contest. I was assigned to guard the former Bibb County player. When I got into the game, Timmy T told me, "Man, don't foul out!" as I had been prone to do, "We need you the whole game." After Alabama's point guard had driven past me three consecutive times, during a time-out, Coach Pritchett yelled, "Flea, I put you in there to slow this guy down!" What he didn't know was, I had picked up on a habit my opponent had. I noticed he would drop his head and fail to look up the court when I yelled out to my teammates which defense we were in. I told Coach Pritchett, "I've got him figured out," to which he replied, "You better or you'll be sitting over here with me!"

I alerted my teammates I was changing our defensive signals. I told them "Blue 21," our man to man full court press, was now "Orange 21," our man to man half court press, and vice versa. In other words, Blue was now our half-court press, and Orange was now our full court press. Lastly, I shared, "When I say 12 instead of 21 we don't press at all. Instead, we get back down the court and into our half-court defense." When play resumed, to further confuse Alabama's point guard, I varied my inflection when calling out which defense we were in. My strategy worked, and I neutralized the point guard for the better part of the ballgame.

At one point, in what had now become a back and forth battle, 'Bama's backup point guard ran me into his teammate, Clevie Joe Parker who had set a "pick" (i.e. a blocking move by an offensive player to free up a teammate) on the play. Parker was like a brick wall, and when I ran into him, my jaw rattled. The pick play with Parker happened again, a few sequences later, and I was slightly shaken up on the play. After I had shaken off the cobwebs, I yelled at my teammates, "Call out the damn pick!" Later, during the second half of the game,

I recognized Alabama was about to run the pick play involving Parker. I turned to my right and took off running to try to beat the player I was guarding to his spot before Parker arrived. I was at about full speed when suddenly I ran into Clevie Joe, whose chest I'd gotten to know quite well by now, and saw lights bulbs flashing as I was falling backward. I thought the flashes were from the bulbs from photographers' cameras. When I hit the hardwood floor, my head bounced a time or two. You could have heard a pin drop in the Coliseum. There was total silence. Our trainer rushed onto the court to aid me. He sat me up and tried using an ammonia capsule to bring me to my senses, but it didn't work. Then he tried a second capsule, and I became somewhat alert. Next, he began testing me for a concussion. The trainer asked, "Flea, do you know where you are? How many fingers do you see?" I answered those and other questions correctly. I asked the trainer what had happened to me. He told me I had been knocked out. As the trainer and one of my teammates walked me back to the bench, there was a round of applause from the fans. When we got to our bench, I pulled away from the trainer and teammate and walked back onto the court. Coach Pritchett said, "Flea, where the hell do you think you're going?" I told him there was no way he was taking me out of the game and if I had to, I would fight every person on the bench including him. After conferring with the trainer to make sure I was okay, Coach let me stay in the game.

When play restarted, one of the referees attempted to throw the basketball to an Alabama player who was about to shoot a free throw. I stepped right in front of him, and to everyone's astonishment, I cursed my teammates out for allowing me to be hit so hard on the pick play. I told them if it happened again I was going to take each one of them one by one and embarrass them in front of 11,000 people by kicking their %$#*! Next, I walked up to the backup point guard, and said, "If you run that play again, I'm going to foul you so hard they're going to have to throw me out of the game!" Sure enough, a few minutes later the guy called for the pick play. This time, I avoided Parker, and as the guard tried to cut to the basket, I hit him with a hard elbow to the chest. The ball popped loose. We went diving for it and slid underneath the draped scorer's table. While hidden by the curtains, the Crimson Tide player and I jostled. I landed a left elbow to his face right before players grabbed us by our ankles to pull us out from underneath the table.

The referees had missed my hard foul on the player, but Alabama fans had taken notice and expressed their disapproval by throwing Coke and popcorn onto the court. The game had to be stopped for several minutes to clean up the floor. After play resumed, as 'Bama's guard was trying to pass the ball inbounds, I barked, "I told you not to run that play again! If you think that was a hard foul, the next one is going to be twice as hard. I'll get thrown out of this game before I let you run that %&$# pick play again!" My scare tactic worked. The guard did not call for the "screen" again the rest of the basketball game.

With minutes left in the contest, we led by one point. Alabama scored a basket to take the lead by one. With about four seconds left in the game, I took an inbound pass and threw the ball three-quarters of the length of the court to Timmy T. He caught the ball in the air and shot it as time expired. The ball bounced on the rim about three or four times and fell harmlessly to the floor. We had lost to the Crimson Tide by one point. Back in the locker room, I held my head in my hands and wept. I had expended so much energy during the contest; I could barely walk to the showers afterward.

GAME 2 AGAINST THE TIDE

The next time we played Alabama was at home in Memorial Coliseum. This time, over 12,000 people watched the basketball game. Like the last one, the contest was an all-out war. The battle see-sawed back and forth with neither team being able to take control. With under four minutes left in the game, we had the lead and victory was within our grasp. Then, the strangest thing happened. One of our players fouled out, and we only had four players left. I thought the contest would end and we would be declared the winner since we had the lead at the time. Per basketball rules, however, a game must continue when such circumstance occurs. I had not known this before. With only four men available, all we could do was play a 2-2 zone defense. We were at an extreme disadvantage now and didn't have a chance playing five against four. Alabama took the lead, held it and ended up winning by six points. It was a tough way to lose against your arch rival. The final score was 81-75. I was devastated once again about losing to the Tide. I'll never forget those games two against Alabama.

Alabama vs. Auburn 1975 JV Box Score

Scholastically, I did well during the school year and finished with a B grade point average. Not long after I had returned home for the summer, I ran into George Pugh who had seen me play against his Tide in the game in Tuscaloosa. He was surprised to learn I was not on scholarship at Auburn. Ensuing, he gave me an Alabama recruiting pitch, so to speak, and suggested I consider transferring to the Capstone where he felt I stood a better chance of being offered a b-ball scholarship. I told him I was happy at Auburn and felt confident a scholarship offer was forthcoming. I also ran into some of the individuals who had laughed and joked about me being too small to make the team at Auburn. Well, you learn a lot about people when you do something they don't think you can do. They lie! I just listened and chuckled inside when they said, "We knew you were going to make it all the time."

SOPHOMORE YEAR ON THE PLAINS

My sophomore year on the Plains was interesting, to say the least. I, 1). Pledged a fraternity. This was something I said I would never do. 2). Went to my Spanish teacher's house to get some information for a test and watched her and her boyfriend smoke marijuana out of a bong pipe. 3). Got into it with a white teammate over his use of the "N-Word," 4.) Nearly got kicked out of school for fighting in a fraternity football game, and 5). Stormed out of basketball practice after scoring 32 points in a scrimmage.

1). Two former High School track All-Americans I met my freshman year, Willie Smith and Gerald Russell, approached me about going to an Omega Psi Phi (aka Que) pledge meeting. I had no intention of pledging, but I went to the meeting with my two friends, out of curiosity. After the meeting, I was still convinced I was not going to pledge a fraternity. Willie, who would go on to win two Olympic Gold Medals, and Gerald however, were able to convince me to pledge with them, and I did. At one point during our indoctrination, they asked me to meet them at the school library. There they talked about quitting the pledge program, but I was able to convince them otherwise. For me, pledging Omega was as challenging and rewarding of an experience as my basketball walk-on one. The three of us "crossed over" the spring of 1976. I had broken a "family tradition," so to speak, in that, by coincidence, both Granddad William and Dad had pledged Alpha Phi Alpha in college. Even though Auburn didn't have an Alpha chapter at the time, Omega was the right choice for me.

2). That semester, I had a Spanish class in which our instructor was a Graduate Assistant. On the first day of class, I sat in the back of the room with three or four other athletes who were also taking the course. The second day of class, the Grad Assistant walked in wearing a see-through blouse. All the athletes walked to the front of the class and we told the male students sitting in the front row, they had to move to the back of the class. Admittedly, I didn't hear one thing the voluptuous Instructor said the entire class! When the basketball team returned from a weeklong road trip, the teacher invited me over to her house to pick up some additional information to study for her final exam. When I arrived, the atmosphere was such I knew she had more on her mind than just providing me with some classroom material. Just when I thought she was about to put a move on me; out walks her boyfriend from another room smoking a joint. The next thing I knew, he and the teacher were smoking marijuana out of a bong pipe and asked me if I wanted to join in. By now, I'm thinking all sorts of crazy things. I'm wondering if the boyfriend wanted me to get high and then sit back and watch the Instructor and I play house, or if both were thinking of a ménage à trois. Not knowing what in the world was going on, I got the hell out of there.

3). We had a 6' 10" scholarship freshman on the Junior Varsity who was so fascinated by the way I played, one day he said to me when we were alone, "Man, you're one bad a-- ni#$a! I love watching you play." I told the frosh, "Look, I know you meant well by what you just said, but you do have to understand that word is offensive to black people. If I let you speak it again around me, especially in front of other black folks, they're going to wonder, "Why would Flea let the frosh say that to Him?" So, going forward, don't use that word around me again. Well, a few practices later, the freshman said the word again in my presence regarding my play. So, I pulled him aside again and reminded him of our previous conversation. I reiterated, "Like I said, man, if you say that word one more time around me, I'm going to have to kick your a#$!"

We had finished a scrimmage one day, and the players were filing into the locker room when the 6' 10" guy goes, "Hey guys, did you see my little ni#$a out there today? My ni#$a knows he can play some ball." I walked up to the freshman, as though I were going to pat him on both shoulders, and wrapped my thumbs around the shoulder straps of his practice jersey. Next, I picked him up in the air, leaned forward and pinned him against his locker. It was reminiscent of what happened to me with Mom. The freshman looked down and saw his feet weren't touching the floor. He was freaked out of his mind. The Coaches walked in, and one said, "Flea, what the hell is going on here?" I barked, "I've warned the freshman two or three times if he ever used that word he just said around me again, I was going to kick his a#$! If anybody comes up to me and tries to stop me, I'm going to do to them what I'm about to do to him." Now, the Coaches were freaking out. Coach Pritchett eventually talked me into letting the player down. My punishment for the locker room incident was I had to run Memorial Coliseum the next day, and run additional suicides after practice.

The next day, while running the Coliseum, I got tired and stopped at one of the top rails to lean over to catch my breath. Recognizing the Coaches weren't paying too much attention to me, I started going halfway down each aisle and then sliding over one or two aisles when they weren't looking. At one point, Coach Pritchett blew his whistle and said, "Flea, are you skipping aisles? If I catch you cheating, you're going to have to run the Coliseum again." I responded, "I can't hear you, Coach. I'm busy running the stairs. I'm running the stairs baby." By the time I was nearly halfway around the Coliseum, all the players and Coaches knew I was skipping aisles and rows, so, it got to be a contest between Coach Pritchett and me as to whether or not he could catch me cheating. In his trying to catch me in the act, the practice had to be stopped for a while because everyone was laughing so hard.

4). The Ques made it to the intramural flag football championship game against the white fraternity that had members riding horses and waving Confederate flags during last year's homecoming. From the get-go, I knew this was going to be an ugly football game. During the contest, some of their guys started making extremely derogatory comments directed at the black female students watching the event. My fraternity brothers and I had had enough. I made a hard block on one of their guys and knocked him on his butt. While getting up off the ground, he said, "What are these ni#$as out here doing?" I tapped him on the shoulder and summarily knocked him out. After that, all my frat brothers sought out a white boy to fight. It was mass chaos. The next day, three members of our fraternity and me were called into the Intramural Sports Director's office. There, the Director informed me he heard I had started the altercation and as a result, faced expulsion from the school. I told him if he tried to do so, I would contact my Dad and one of his friends who was a State Senator and between the two men, they would have his job by the next day. I got up and walked out of the Director's office. He called me back in and told us he would do more research on what happened that day. He should have done that before bringing us into his office and being accusatory in the first place! I called Dad and explained to him what happened. I told him I had used his and the Senator's name as a bluff. He shared it wasn't a problem, and if it turned out I did need him and the Legislator to intervene, they would be more than happy to do so. A few days later, my frat brothers and I were called back into the Director's office. He told us we were correct about how the events unfolded and that the other fraternity had been put on probation. We were exonerated, and I didn't get expelled from school.

5). That season, the Coaching staff brought in a 6' 2" guard who had played in the Big Ten conference. The first time I saw him play, I couldn't believe he had gotten a scholarship over me. We had a scrimmage one day, and he was on the opposing team. To drive home a point to the Coaches and the player, I took the poor guy "to school." I was unmerciful against him. When I scored my 28th point, one of the Assistant Coaches told me to stop shooting. Following, I ran a play designed for one of our big men to take the shot, but the guy I was trying to pass to was guarded. Wide open at the top of the key, I took and made the shot. The Assistant Coach went ballistic and told me if I took one more shot he was sending my a#$ to the showers. Several sequences later, the identical thing happened. The Assistant Coach stopped the scrimmage, called me over and chewed me out. I asked him why he got on me more than he did any other player. He told me, "The day I stop getting on you Flea; that's the day I stop caring about you." I wasn't buying it at the time and started disrobing on my way to the locker room. I made my mind up; I was walking out in my birthday suit! When I realized a few fans were watching the scrimmage, I kept my shorts and jock strap on. I grabbed my things and headed back to the apartment with no intention of returning to the team. The next day, I didn't go to practice. That evening, my phone rang, and it was Mike Wilson. I told him I knew the Coaches had put him up to calling me because they knew he was probably the only guy that could talk me into coming back at that juncture. Mike and I talked for a while. Red got me to calm down and convinced me to rejoin the team. I told him to tell the Coaches I would come back but only under one condition. I would not run the Coliseum, but I would be willing to run additional suicides. Mike hung up the phone and called me back about an hour later. He told me the Coaches said I would have to do the "stairs" of the Coliseum and run additional suicides. My negotiating skills weren't quite as strong as I thought.

That basketball season, I played on the Junior Varsity again, but this time I started the entire season. I improved my scoring average to 12 points per game. After one game, against a Junior College (aka JUCO), their Head Coach approached me and asked me If I would be willing to transfer to his school. He told me he thought I could be an All-American in his program. I couldn't believe an opposing Coach would be bold enough to recruit me right on my home floor. He didn't realize I was already a sophomore and would have been ineligible to play at the JUCO level. I thanked the coach for his offer and told him I was happy where I was.

The funniest thing that happened to me that season was when we played the number one ranked Junior College in the nation. I was having a terrific game until I threw a no-look-behind-the-back pass to Red who missed the ball. Following, it hit a popcorn stand in the lobby, then bounced out an open door on the side of the gym, and into the parking lot. A young boy returned the ball and handed it to a referee. I heard the buzzer sound and knew Coach Pritchett was taking me out of the game. I didn't look at him as I ran past him because I feared his wrath. I sat on the very end of the bench to get as far away from Coach as I possibly could. As he was pacing the sideline, he came down to the end of the bench, with his veins about to burst in his head. He shouted, "Flea!! Whenever you're in a game, and you are behind in points, don't you ever, and I mean ever, throw a behind-the-back no look pass again. Do you understand me?" I replied, "Yes sir!" He said, "Now get your a#$ back in the game!"

During the season, some spot-on articles were written about my play. One was in the Montgomery Advertiser, and the other was in the Auburn Plainsman entitled, "It doesn't matter how small." The writer wrote, "He has the ball handling finesse of Eddie Johnson (our All-American guard), scores about 12 points per game, shoots 50% from the field, and he plays on the Auburn Junior varsity. Any particular reason? But Simmons thinks it's solely because of his height, and many tend to agree with him." The writer went on to pen,

"Simmons, a sophomore ... stands 5-9, not very tall, even for a guard, but as the old cliché goes, he makes up for it with desire ... if confidence plays any part in determining whether Simmons will make the varsity, he has more than enough. It isn't the brash, cock style of confidence, but rather the "I know I can do it if I try hard enough" style." The writer was spot on! He was talking about Mom's "seeds" and my "Little Train" that could mentality– no doubt!

After the end of the season, players had their exit interviews with Coach Bob. The purpose of these meetings was to review the player's season and discuss things to work on during the summer. Coach Bob and I spoke for a while, and he told me he thought I had an excellent season. I asked him if I had performed well enough to earn a scholarship. He informed me he thought I might be too small for the SEC. Immediately, I was thinking, "What the hell do you think I've been doing the past two years?" He asked me who I would guard when we played Alabama's varsity - Anthony Murray or T.R. Dunn? I told him Murray and said we could also play a zone defense against Alabama like Tennessee had done, during the season, with their diminutive 5' 9" guard Johnny Darden. I reminded Coach that Tennessee had finished third in the conference that year - ahead of Auburn. *My can of whip a#$ seed was sprouting out of my mouth now.* He went on to tell me he felt I was the best player in the state of Alabama under 6 feet that year, including Alabama's incoming freshman Kent Looney who was the High School Player of the Year in the state. I walked out of the room devastated. Several Varsity

152

players, who were waiting outside Coach's office for their exit interviews, could only shake their head in disbelief over what they had overheard, as I walked out the door.

JUNIOR YEAR, FALL SEMESTER

During the fall semester of my junior year, I made the Varsity basketball team. We were only days away from starting the season and flying out to Dallas to play in a tournament at Southern Methodist University (SMU). I was playing one-on-one against teammate Stan Pietkiewicz in the auxiliary gym when I stepped on his foot after grabbing a rebound and suffered a severe high ankle sprain. Subsequently, a gel cast had to be placed on my foot and ankle. Unable to travel to SMU with the team, I found myself sitting alone in my apartment with my thoughts. I had put up better numbers, scoring-wise, my sophomore year than scholarship players brought in since I had been on the squad, and yet I was not on scholarship. It made no sense to me. I came to realize college sports was a business. It took time and money to recruit a player, and Coaches hoped to get a return on their investment. If the investment didn't pan out, having the luxury of a player on their team, like me, who was playing for free, was icing on the cake. I also thought long and hard about the sacrifices my mother was making just to try to keep me in school. Although I was taking out student loans, the amount of money I was borrowing was increasing at a rapid rate. After some serious soul searching, I decided transferring to Auburn University at Montgomery (AUM) would be the best thing to do for Mom and me. By attending AUM, I would be able to live at home, thereby reducing my room and board expense, and I could walk on to the Senators' fledgling basketball program which was in its second year of infancy.

Before Christmas Break, I received a call from Charlie Thomas who was a black DJ on Auburn's student radio station. He co-hosted a program with Sylvia Little geared towards black students at the school. Charlie invited me to be a guest on a segment about the life of a walk-on athlete at Auburn. I gladly accepted. The other guest on the show was my former roommate Mike McCloud who had gone on to earn a football scholarship.

During my part of the interview, I shared my various experiences during my two years as a walk-on. My hosts were unaware of the trials and tribulations of a walk-on. I spoke about not having shoes my size available after making the team, not having access to tutors or meals at the athletic dorm and more. The show stopper came when I pulled out the Junior Varsity stats for the previous season. The information showed I was the second leading scorer on the squad at 12 points per game and had outscored every scholarship player on the Junior Varsity, excluding a Varsity player who only played two games on the Junior Varsity. The team's statistics for the scholarship players, when compared to mine, stunned the hosts of the show.

Charlie an avid basketball fan, who had seen me play numerous times, couldn't believe I wasn't on scholarship and said so during the broadcast. Sylvia who had also seen me play, couldn't believe I wasn't on scholarship either. After sharing with them my exit interview conversation with Coach Bob the previous season, Sylvia started crying over the airwaves and Charlie got so choked up, he had to compose himself to speak. After regaining her composure, Sylvia asked me why I felt I wasn't on scholarship. I didn't mince words. I said, "It's because I'm black!" I went on to say, "If you look around the SEC, schools have a quota regarding the number of blacks on each basketball team. Just look at our team." My words had to have sent shockwaves through the airwaves. I had done the unthinkable. I had spoken about racial disparity on Auburn's team and in the powerful Southeastern Conference. Any logical person knew I was telling the truth. The problem was, nobody wanted to talk about it or admit it. Using my personal circumstance and experience, I had brought out something that was taboo, front and center!

After hearing the broadcast, several black students approached me the next day at school and told me they were going to boycott the basketball program to get me put on scholarship. I told them my honesty over the air probably made things worse for me and more than likely killed my scholarship chance. I also told them that considering the fact they had seen me play for 2 years and knew I was a walk-on, they should have put pressure on the basketball program long before now. I thanked them for their concern and asked them not to boycott. After my radio interview, I knew it was in my best interest to get out of "Dodge." When I got home for Christmas break, I informed Mom I was going to enroll at Auburn University at Montgomery. Later, I met with their basketball Head Coach and started assisting the team that season.

Chapter 15

Transitioning to AUM

That fall semester at the main campus, I was thinking about a pre-dentistry major. During a meeting with my guidance counselor at AUM, I confided I probably wouldn't be happy in the field of Dentistry. As we discussed what I thought I wanted to do after college, the guidance counselor asked me if I'd ever thought about business as a career. I remember laughing and saying, "Business courses are easy. I prefer something more challenging." The advisor shot back, "Butch, what fuels the nation's economy?" I said, "Business." Then the counselor said, "There you go!" It was at that point; I changed my major to Business. This change caused me to lose some credit hours. To achieve my goal of graduating in four years, I was faced with having to buckle down on my academics and go to summer school for the first time. That semester I took 15 hours and the following semesters I took 20 hours in course work each semester.

The AUM Senators were members of the National Association of Intercollegiate Athletics (NAIA). Back then, student-athletes who transferred were required to sit out one year of competition but could practice with their new team. So, I began practicing with AUM's squad, of which I knew nearly half of the players. My cousin Cut Rate, and his best friend Larry Woolfolk (aka Wolf) were starters on the team along with Doc and Timmy T who had transferred the year before I arrived. Two other former Auburn University players (Ray Woodard and Bill Wallace) were also on the team. I also knew a few other players, like Thad Fitzpatrick. When the squad played, I would help keep stats and drive one of the vans to away games.

That summer, I managed to land a part-time job with RadioShack in Eastdale Mall which had recently opened. I was a sales clerk, and I also helped replenish the inventory. It was great experience and unbeknownst to me; I began honing my sales skills at the time. Academically, I thoroughly enjoyed my business courses, particularly Business Statistics, and Marketing. I was fond of Business Stats because it was analytical in nature, like me. Marketing offered some cool classes. I learned why certain items are placed where they are in grocery stores and why companies develop certain products for certain market groups. For example, two major manufacturers of bar-b-que sauce catered to different markets for particular "palate related" reasons. One company did not add extra ingredients to its sauce because their data indicated black people liked adding their own ingredients such as honey or lemons or onions, as an example. The other company focused primarily on white people's taste buds. I did very well that semester and made Dean's List, as I would go on to do multiple times.

Chapter 16

How I Met My Wife

That summer, Mom and I moved into a house on Briarbrook Court which was on the main street in Brookview. There, she and I met Reverend Calvin Chambers, his wife Isrealean, and their seven children: Annette, Calvin Jr., Johnnie Mae, Willie Dell, Doris (Mimi), Elvis, and Jacqualine. Mom and I developed a relationship with the family that extends to this day. Mom and Mrs. Chambers grew to be best friends. Shortly after we moved, there were several occasions when I couldn't find Mom and had no idea where she was. I came to learn she would be at the Chambers' house. Every day, after work, Mom would go down to the Chambers' abode. Whenever Mom needed a ride to the store, you name it; Mrs. Chambers was always there for her. Sometimes I would catch the two of them giggling and behaving just like teenage girls. Goodness knows they enjoyed one another. I was glad to see Mom in such a happy state when they were together.

As for me, things at school were going great, and I was coming into my own in basketball. The game had slowed down in my mind, and everything was coming easier to me. I could "call my shot" as soon as it left my fingertips and would say "bucket" while the ball was in the air because I knew the shot was true. I was 5' 9", 157 pounds and in the best physical condition of my life. I was brimming with confidence on and off the court and determined to have my self-assuredness translate into success with the ladies. To that end, I began working on my "new" pickup line. One night, as I was diligently practicing my new "Intro" in the bathroom mirror, I decided to use my new "rap" on the next woman I met that caught my eye. Part of my line was, "You're like sunshine, (long pause) you brighten up my day." I added some other words to my repertoire and felt good-to-go. You couldn't convince me I wasn't a cold blooded "Chick Magnet" that evening. Later that night, I got a call from Cut Rate informing me there was going to be a "Serious Run" (i.e. when the best players go against one another) at AUM the next day. That morning, after I got dressed, I opened the sports section of the Montgomery Advertiser and lo and behold my recent interview with the paper was in it. I headed over to AUM with one "big head" and wearing short shorts so the chicks could check out my ripped thighs.

When I walked up to the outer doors of the gymnasium, I had my basketball bag on my left shoulder, and I was "profiling." I pulled on one of the doors, but it was locked. Another door was open and the "much too full of himself" Flea entered his "domain." As I walked through the lobby towards the inside doors of the gym, I stopped to admire myself in the glass of the school's trophy cases. In the mirror and to my left, I saw this drop dead gorgeous girl sitting on the steps reading a book. "What an opportunity to use my new line," I thought. I walked up to the young lady and said, "Hi, I'm Butch Simmons. You've probably heard of me. You know, Auburn University

160

basketball. I'm the guy that's in the newspaper today." The young lady replied, "Never heard of you. Plus, I like football anyway." Not to be denied the opportunity to use my new line, I said, "No problem. I must say, though, "You're just like sunshine, and you've just brightened up my day." I kept talking and rapping thinking everything I was saying was super cool. All of a sudden, the young lady burst into laughter, leaned over and was chuckling so hard she was nearly in tears. I was speechless. After what seemed like forever for the beautiful coed to compose herself, I said, "Was it that bad?" She replied, "Worse!" Totally humbled, I said, "Do you mind if I start all over?" The beautiful young lady said, "Well, it can't get any worse." I began by saying, "Please allow me to reintroduce myself. I'm Eric Simmons, and I just tried to be something and someone that I'm not. That other guy you just met, is not me." I don't recall the rest of the conversation because I was so star struck looking at the woman. For me, it was love at first sight. I asked the young lady for her telephone number, but she would not give it to me. She did tell me her name was Cynthia Derico. I went inside the gym motivated by the angel I had just met and proceeded to annihilate players in the gymnasium.

When I got home that night, I couldn't get the young lady out of my mind. Figuring I might never see her again, I decided to look in the white pages of the telephone directory to try to find her number. I started alphabetically and was intent on calling every Derico in the phone book if need be. I had probably called about 30 people and had the same result which was, "I'm sorry you've got the wrong number." I had been on the phone for quite some time and said to myself, "I'll make one more call and then try again tomorrow." I dialed my last number for the day and said, "Hello, I'm trying to reach Cynthia Derico. Is she available?" The young lady who answered the phone replied, "Yes, she's here, I'll go get her." My heart was beating 100 miles an hour. I couldn't believe I had found her. My heartthrob answered the phone, and I said, "Hi, this is Butch Simmons, the guy you met at AUM's gym today." Surprised, she said, "How did you get this number?" I said, "You gave it to me." To which she replied, "No, I didn't!" I confessed and told her I had been calling all the Dericos in the phone book and was determined to keep trying until I found her. There was total silence. I imagine she was shocked a complete stranger would scroll through the telephone book searching for her. I assured the co-ed I wasn't crazy and told her I just wanted to get to know her better. Although she let me speak for a little while, Cynthia made it clear she already had a boyfriend and was not interested in anyone else. After we hung up, I still couldn't get her out of my mind.

Cynthia Derico

Unconvinced she was happy in her current relationship, I continued trying to talk to her but continued to be rejected. On one call, Cynthia recommended I try talking to a young lady whom she had heard liked me. I set out to prove to Ms. Derico I could get any girl I wanted and so, I started dating her recommendee. I went out of my way to make sure Cynthia saw me with my new girlfriend every chance I got. It turned out my dating someone else didn't bother her, as I hoped it would, in the least. To compound matters, my new girlfriend knew I wanted to be with Cynthia and so, things fizzled out between us. This was at the time when an AUM basketball player and I were looking out from a balcony onto the school's courtyard and spotted Cynthia headed to class. I said, "You see that young lady right there. One day she's going to be my wife." To which the ball player replied, "There's no way you're going to get that girl. No way!" "Wanna bet? Watch me," I retorted. Eventually, Cynthia and her boyfriend broke up. It took some time afterward, but eventually, we started dating.

The first time I went over to the Derico house I had the opportunity to meet her father, Limmor Sr. and seven of her eight siblings; Gwen, Mary Ann, Reola, Connie, twins Juanita and Darlnita, and Limmor (Junior) Jr. Her oldest sister Charlestine was married. She and her husband, Tilman had their own place. Cynthia's mother had passed away before we started dating. As I watched Cynthia and her siblings walking about, I remember thinking to myself, "Man, this is a good-looking family." I already knew Gwen, Mary Ann, and Reola somewhat due to having gone to Robert E. Lee with them.

Whenever I would call Cynthia, I would keep her on the phone so long she would fall asleep. I later learned, sometimes she would go to bed and hand the phone to her younger sister Connie. That's unfortunate for Cynthia because Connie got to hear some of my best "lines." Because they were so close and comical together, I called the two of them Frick and Frack. Cynthia's and my love began to grow, and after about a year of dating, I proposed to her. She accepted my request to be married. Marriage was a big step for both of us, especially her because she was only 19.

When I finally got the courage to sit down with her Dad to ask him for his daughter's hand in marriage, I was nervous as all get out. Cynthia and I sat on the sofa across from her father, and after he and I had some small chit chat, I said, "Mr. Derico, I'd like to ask you for your daughter's hand in marriage." There was total silence. Pop, as he was called, looked at Cynthia and then looked at me and didn't say a word. The silence was excruciating. It seemed as if an hour had gone by and there was nothing but silence. I remember thinking to myself, "If Pop says no, then I'll call Cynthia and ask her to climb out her bedroom window and elope with me." Just as I had finished thinking about my backup plan, Pop looked at Cynthia and said, "Baby are you sure you want to do this?" The love of my life replied, "Yes Daddy, I'm sure." I was relieved, but then, Mr. Derico went silent on us again. He probably was still mulling things over. Unable to deal with the quietness any longer, I said, "Mr. Derico, I know how important it is to you that Cynthia finishes college, so you have my word I will make sure she completes her education. I will even pay for it myself." Without hesitating Pop said, "You two have my blessing." My future bride and I were elated. I was so excited I was about to kiss her when she pushed me back and gave me a look with her eyes reminding me her Dad was still in the room. Years later, I thought about that day with my future father-in-law and wondered if my saying I would pay for my wife's remaining two years of college had influenced him to allow us to get married. If that were the case, then all I can say is Pop was one heck of a poker player because he sure called my hand.

My senior year at AUM, I made the basketball team. Eligibility wise I was a Junior because of having sat out the previous season. I was looking forward to getting back out on the hardwood. The Senators' Head Coach had taken a job at a Division II school over the summer, and a new coach was brought in. He ran the University of North Carolina's four corners offense of which I was no big fan. The premise behind the attack was to put four men on the corners of the offensive end of half court and have the point guard set up plays from near half court. The strategy was to slow the game down, and I felt I was much better suited for a fast break, up-tempo, style of play. Grudgingly, I decided to hang up my basketball shoes. I had something more to play for in my life, and it was my bride to be Cynthia. That fall, I played in a basketball tournament in Monroeville, Alabama with Cut Rate, Wolf, and some other guys and averaged about

32 points per game. Word got back to the AUM Coaching staff, and the Assistant Coach asked me to rejoin the team. I declined the offer. Giving up basketball was probably the hardest thing I had ever done in my life up to that point. I had worked so hard over the years and poured my heart and soul into the game. Few people realize how difficult it is for an athlete to let go of the game he/she loves. That's why we see so many athletes come out of retirement and try to make a comeback. I cried so hard for two days about the realization my playing days were over, I almost became ill.

Me (10), Doc (35) and Timmy T (40)

To prepare for the rigors of taking 20 hours a semester, I developed a plan whereby after class, I would spend the most time studying my hardest subject, say an hour and a half, then one hour on my next most challenging course. Following, I would take a 30-minute break and then spend 45 minutes on the third hardest course, and 30 minutes studying the fourth toughest, etc. I did this three semesters religiously and made Dean's List each time. I achieved my goal of graduating in four years (and one semester). I graduated with a Bachelor of Science degree in Business Administration with a major in Management and a minor in Marketing. I missed graduating Cum Laude by 0.01 of a point. The Dean of the School of Business called me to his office one day and invited me to enter the school's Master of Business Administration (MBA) program and told me I would be accepted irrespective of my score on the Graduate Requisite Exam (GRE). I thanked the Dean for his incredible offer and explained to him I was about to get married and needed to go ahead and find a job.

Chapter 17

Bachelor's Party and Wedding

The fact that I don't remember very much about my bachelor's party is proof I had a good one! I do know my future brother-in-law's Joshua (Josh) Lykes, Mary's husband, and Benny Holt, Gwen's husband, took me out and we had a great time! I vaguely recall going to a night club in Josh's hometown of Verbena, Alabama and turning off onto a dirt road where there was a club far back in the woods. As best as I recall, I think we got to my house somewhere between 3 and 4 A.M. the morning of my wedding. I was so out of it, I passed out on the sofa in the living room. When Mom woke me up early that morning, my head was pounding. I remember thinking to myself, "Man, there's no way I'm going to make it through the day, let alone get married." I was in such a bad way; Mom pulled out all sorts of old remedies to get me sobered up. After eating a ton of greasy food, and drinking only goodness know what, I finally started feeling much better several hours before the wedding.

Cynthia and I got married on August 18, 1979. She was born and raised a Baptist and attended King Hill Baptist Church. Born and baptized a Methodist, I had been attending St. John's African Methodist Episcopal (AME) Church. We agreed to have both our Pastors take part in our wedding ceremony. When I got to the church, my best man Doug Sanders, whom I had met at Auburn, was there to meet me along with the other groomsmen who were Doc, Limmor Jr., Benny, Josh, and Melvin Ware, Reola's fiancé. Cynthia's bridal party consisted of Charlestine, Gwen, Mary Ann, Reola, Connie and her good friend Laletta Frazier. The ring bearer was a cute kid from my church named Carlos, and the flower girls were Cynthia's adorable little twin sisters Juanita and Darlnita.

I waited in a side room of King Hill Baptist Church with Cynthia's Pastor, Reverend James Bozeman and my Pastor, Anderson Todd. About 20 minutes after the scheduled start of the wedding, Cynthia had not arrived. Both clergymen began to fidget, and this made me even more nervous than I already was. Roughly another 5 to 10 minutes had passed, it seemed, and one of the men of "The Cloth" said, "We may have a no show." I began sweating profusely and fearing the worse. I started wondering if Cynthia had gotten cold feet and had backed out of the wedding. Just as I was reaching a point of extremely high anxiety, someone said, "The bride's here!" I don't think I had ever been more relieved in my life.

When Cynthia walked through the door with Pop, she was more beautiful than the first day I met her. She looked like an angel as she walked down the aisle. My heart was pounding and bursting with pride. As we turned to take our wedding vows, one of my Cousins, from Georgia, who had apparently started celebrating the wedding early yelled, "Kiss the bride!" The church erupted into laughter. When we got to the part where the Pastor said, "Cynthia, do you promise to love honor and obey?" Cynthia didn't say a word. I looked at her with my eyes trying to encourage her to repeat the phrase. Still, she remained quiet and looked at me as though she were mad about something. Now I'm really beginning to sweat. It dawned on me, and everyone in the church, Cynthia was having a big problem with saying the word – "Obey." With everyone watching us, under my breath I said to my bride to be, "It's okay to say, Obey." Then she gave me "that look." Reluctantly, and barely audible, Cynthia finally whispered, "Obey."

Wedding Photos

After the wedding, we had our reception at Cynthia's house. By this time, our honeymoon night was my focus! I was more locked in than I'd ever been in basketball. I tried very hard to get my new bride to drink champagne, fully knowing she didn't drink alcohol. She knew what I was up to though and would have none of my giddiness. Hours later, after everyone left, I was ready to settle down and get some sleep when my new bride said, "Now we can head to Atlanta for our honeymoon." I couldn't believe my ears. I was still hung over from my Bachelor's Party and dog-tired from our Wedding Day. I told my bride I was too tired to try to make the 3 and 1/2-hour drive and asked if it would be okay to leave the next morning. The look in her eyes was one of total disappointment. I couldn't stand to see her unhappy, especially on her wedding day, so, I told her we would go ahead and head to Atlanta. When we reached Opelika, I decided to get off I-85 and drive through a McDonalds to buy a large cup of coffee to keep me awake. Less than a mile after I was back on the interstate, I spilled the cup of boiling-hot coffee right in my lap. I screamed and almost ran off the road. After checking my crown jewels to ensure they were okay, I thought to myself, "Well I'm wide awake now."

As wedding gifts, Titus and Regina took care of all our activities in Atlanta, and Jeremiah let us spend the week in his new house. After we had settled in at Jake's house, I sprung from the shower with a pep in my step. It was honeymoon night! Bless her heart; Cynthia was so tired from her wedding day, she fell sound asleep. I sat on the bed and just watched her, and thanked God for bringing her into my life. Over the new few days, Cynthia and I had a blast in "Hot 'Lanta." Our activities included riding the lift to the top of Stone Mountain and spending the day at the park, going to the zoo, and eating dinner at the revolving restaurant overlooking the city.

Chapter 18

My Corporate Career

SOUTH CENTRAL BELL

During my senior year at AUM, part of my job search strategy was to interview with three to four companies I had moderate interest in so that I could hone my interviewing skills for businesses that were of my primary interest. This was the "Pre-game Preparation seed" I learned from Mom. During the second semester, I received a phone call from a Recruiter with South Central Bell, AT&T's most profitable "Baby Bell." The Recruiter told me I had an impressive resume and he noticed I had played basketball at Auburn. He shared, he had graduated from Auburn around the same time I was there but had not heard of an Eric Simmons on the basketball team. I told him I didn't play under my first name, but used my nickname, Butch, instead. The interviewer said, "Flea, this is TG!" I couldn't believe it. I was speaking with Thom Gossom, who was an upperclassman and former walk-on who became a standout wide receiver at Auburn. He was the first black athlete in the Southeastern Conference to walk-on, earn a full scholarship and graduate. TG had become a mentor to me, especially during my crucial freshman year, during my time on the Plains. He was also Timmy T's brother-in-law at the time. Thom conducted a thorough interview with me over the phone. The session went so well, he offered me a managerial position, on the spot, with the company. My following "in person" interview with my prospective Manager was merely a formality. In my view, it was a gift from God to have an Auburn man call me out of the blue, and hire me into my first job after college.

After moving to Birmingham, Cynthia began classes at the University of Alabama at Birmingham (UAB), and I started working in South Central Bell's Main and Toll Frame Central Office (CO). The facility was reputed to be the largest in the entire Bell System and was the first in the nation to implement Electronic Switching System (ESS) technology (i.e. digital transmission using computer control). I was a "First Line" Manager Trainee working with a female Manager. Jointly, we supervised 12 female Union employees.

My subordinates did not welcome me with open arms. I was a "kid" fresh out of college, in their view, and several employees felt they had been passed over by Management with my hire. Plus, upcoming negotiations between the Union (Communications Workers of America or CWA) and management was looming. The meetings were expected to be contentious, and it was rumored the Union might walk out and go on strike for higher pay.

During my Managerial training at the Main and Toll Frame, I had to learn how to manually trace telephone calls in our Mechanical Relay Switching office, which was more than the length of a football field and about as wide. I also had to go to Chicago for various Technical and Management classes, all of which were graded. By the end of my training, I had to be proficient in doing the work of a Central Office Union employee and be capable of successfully managing a CO.

My Union subordinates tested me early on, often, and at every turn. They would make excuses for taking long lunches, being late, or not doing assigned work by using reasons such as, "It's that time of the month" as justification, and for which I had no counter. One day, I received a call from Headquarters to have what's called a "Special Circuit" run for Ronald Reagan, who was running for President at the time and his staff. These types of "Circuits" were "Private" and "High Priority" in Bell System lexicon. I used to think of them as, "Top Secret Private Lines." Pressed for time to complete the project, I went to my second-best employee to have her wire the necessary circuits. She adamantly refused to do the work. She cursed me out several times and each time I kept my cool. She felt I was giving her extra, and unnecessary, work over other employees. I assured her that was not the case, and shared, her peers had as much on their work plate, at the time, as she. I told her she was the best I had in quickly running "Special Circuits" and in the interest of time, I needed her expertise to run the private lines for the Presidential candidate. Ultimately, the employee settled down and ran the circuits. Afterward, she informed me she was filing a grievance with the Union. Immediately, I called my superior, John Akers, who had been in the Bell System for over 30 years and who was a master in dealing with the CWA and in Union negotiations, to meet with him to discuss what had taken place.

Several days later, Mr. Akers and I met with the employee and the CWA's Local Representative. Right out of the gate, the employee verbally attacked me and accused me of harassing her into doing a task while she was already working on another assignment. Next, she falsified the events as they had occurred. Seeing I was getting riled up, Mr. Akers grabbed my right knee, underneath the table, to try and keep it from continuing to shake uncontrollably. Out of nowhere, in walked a woman whom the employee and I did not know. It turns out she was a visiting Manager who had been touring the facility that past week and had seen and heard the entire interaction between the employee and me. When my turn came to speak, I explained to the Union Representative what had transpired, the reason for my request, and mentioned my repeated attempts to ensure the employee she was not doing additional and unnecessary work. I also shared, I had informed the employee my primary reason for coming to her was because I felt she was the most capable individual to do the job under the circumstance.

After the visiting Manager had corroborated my story, the union employee broke down crying because she knew she didn't have a leg to stand on. Mr. Akers informed me the employee had clearly been insubordinate and there were grounds for dismissal. He asked me what I wanted to do. I told him I felt the employee was a valuable asset to the company and recommended she receive one week off without pay versus termination. The employee lunged across the table trying to get to me and threatened to have her husband come to the office and take care of me. At that juncture, the Union Representative took the employee outside to cool off and informed her she was lucky I hadn't fired her. When they returned, the employee apologized and thanked me for not terminating her. After the employee had left the meeting to go home, the CWA Representative told Mr. Akers, the visiting Manager, and me he had never seen anything like the way I had handled his irate fellow Union member. He commended me on my professionalism and told Mr. Akers I was wise beyond my years. He also thanked me for not firing the employee, which he said I would have been more than justified in doing. Mom's "be professional in your business interactions seed" was taking root. Not long after the meeting, Mr. Akers placed me in the company's "Fast Track" Management Training Program and promoted me to "Second Level" Manager.

Working for South Central Bell was a cool job for a just turned 23-year-old college grad. Mr. Akers was great to work for, and I learned a lot watching him in various negotiations with the CWA. Every time I had the opportunity to drive his company car and was at a stoplight, I would make sure the person next to me saw me on the mobile telephone, which was just reaching the market. Of course, no one would be on the other line when I placed the phone to my ear, but it didn't matter because I was "styling" and "profiling." Another neat thing about working for Ma Bell was, the pay and benefits were excellent.

After my second year with South Central Bell, the strain of managing 12 employees had begun to wear on me. Also, I felt something was missing in my career. Gradually, I began to get the "sales itch." Something was intriguing about the field, and when I looked at myself introspectively, my personality seemed well-suited for the occupation. With South Central not having any open sales jobs at the time, I updated my resume and began interviewing outside companies. I interviewed several businesses, to brush up on my interviewing skills, before sending my resume to my "target company" which was IBM.

IBM

In 1982, IBM was the only non-automotive or petroleum based company in the top 10 of Fortune Magazine's Fortune 500 listing. Ranked at number eight on Fortune's list, the company had $29.1 billion in revenues and was second in profit at $3.31 billion. IBM was the place to be, particularly if you wanted to sell. Admiration for the company was so high, trying to get hired on in sales was extremely difficult. I managed to get an interview at IBM's branch office in Birmingham. There, over a span of several hours, three different Sales Managers interviewed me on the day. Less than a week later, I was offered a Sales Trainee position with the company. To my knowledge, I became the first black male Sales Trainee in the history of the

Birmingham Branch's Data Processing Division (DPD). DPD was
IBM's biggest money maker and the conduit through which its "Big
Iron" mainframe computers were sold. I used to say, "DPD is where
the Big Boys play."

IBM was extremely meticulous about who it chose for its Sales
Training program. Back then, many of the Sales Reps and Sales
Managers had Computer Science, Engineering, and MBA degrees.
Most of my Sales Training program colleagues were Ivy League
graduates, former athletes with stellar grade point averages or
nonathletes with the same. We also had a black Rhodes Scholar, a
UCLA Ph.D., and a former National Football League tight end in my
class. IBM's Sales Training program was so highly regarded, from a
technical standpoint, it was viewed as equivalent to Harvard's MBA in
Computer Science. From a pure Sales Training standpoint, the
program was widely regarded as the best in Corporate America. And
boy, was it intense. I actually saw people break down and cry from the
stress, present party included (once in my apartment bathroom).
"How IBM Teaches Techies to Sell" touches on the Program's
intensity, at the time. At "Big Blue," you had to be able to "walk the
walk and talk the talk." I once shared with Cynthia, working for IBM
was like going to church every day. Dark suits, white shirts, wing tips
and no alcohol. If you had a martini at lunch with a customer, you
best not go back to the office for you risked termination (per the
company's Business Conduct Guidelines) back then. When I went
through it, the Sales Training program was one year in duration and

required a grade point average of 75 or higher to achieve successful completion. Over the course of the year, we spent one month in the branch office, then one to two months in the company's new sales training facility in the Las Colinas suburb of Irving, Texas, and repeated the process throughout the year.

My first class in Las Colinas, consisted of roughly 40 students who hailed from institutions and entities such as Harvard, Duke, Yale, the Wharton School of Business, Wellesley and non-Ivy League schools such as UCLA, Michigan State, Auburn (me), and the (NFL) to name some. When the Class Manager introduced himself to the class, he told us we were amongst the top 10% brightest minds in America. He also revealed, IBM purposefully sought out former athletes because they are familiar with things like understanding the value of hard work, perseverance, and teamwork. Sounded like a Mom "seed" to me. Talk about being pumped up after his introduction to the class. I was ready to go!

During my second class in Texas, a black female graduate of Michigan State approached me and told me several people in the class were going to nominate me for Class President. Being named Class President was the most prestigious honor that could be bestowed on an IBM Sales Trainee. At that time, every CEO of IBM, save Tom Watson, Jr., son of the founder of the company, had been President of their Sales Training class. It was a big deal! When my time came to give my nomination speech, I used IBM's three core values, which were, **E**xcellence in each and everything we do, **C**ustomer Service, and

Respect for the Individual as backdrops for my speech. After stepping to the podium, I thanked the class for considering me to be their Class President. Then, I turned to the blackboard, took a piece of chalk, and wrote the letters E R I C vertically. I used the first letter of the companies three core principles and included the letter **I** to talk about Integrity. Because I had written the letters vertically, at first glance, you couldn't tell I had spelled out my name. It wasn't until I concluded my speech and circled the four letters E R I C and said, "When you add it all up it spells ERIC for Class President" could the viewer realize I had spelled my name. You could have heard a pin drop in the room. The Ivy Leaguers were shocked to see such creativity come out of a black man. They realized they had been so focused on the "core principals," that I had intentionally sent a subliminal message to them, like movie theaters used to do by flashing popcorn between film splices to entice the audience to get up and go buy popcorn and Coca-Cola. Subsequently, I lost the Presidential race by a landslide! Later, I asked the black female Michigan State grad what happened as to why I had lost, and she said, "That was too powerful. They weren't ready for that. Several of us are going to nominate you again for the next class, but next time you're going to have to tone it down if you want to win." In other words, "No More Hot Dogging."

In preparing for my third class, I had to do a mock sales presentation with my Sales Manager. When I completed the presentation, the Manager told me I had done the poorest job he had seen from an IBM Sales Trainee in his entire career. Previous vibes I had gotten from him led me to believe he didn't feel blacks belonged in IBM and weren't competent enough to sell IBM's prized and most profitable product line, "Computer Systems." I was pissed! I kept my composure with the man and left my presentation exactly as it was for my next class, except I reversed the last two pages. When I gave the presentation in Las Colinas, it was regarded by the black Sales Manager I presented to, as the best he had ever seen in the Sales Training program. His opinion, as compared to my Sales Manager's, was as different as "Night" and "Day," no pun intended. That class, I was nominated for Class President again. This time, after thanking the class for their consideration, I recited the poem, "It Couldn't Be Done" by Edgar A. Guest. The poem is my favorite because it sums up my life. During my recital, I replaced the word "he" with the word "we" to make the poem sound inclusive of the entire class. A snippet of what I narrated was, "Somebody said that it couldn't be done, but "we" with a chuckle replied, that maybe it couldn't but "we" would be one who wouldn't say so until "we" tried. Somebody scoffed, oh you'll never do that, at least no one has ever done it, but "we" took off our coat and "we" took off our hat and the first thing they knew "we'd" begun it..." In all honesty, in reciting the poem, I was sending the class and Instructors a message about me. It was, "If you think I'm not going to be successful in this training program and that I'm not going to be your Class President then you better think again, because I'm going to do both. I'm not backing down or giving up." Mom's "seed" relating to "standing firm in your conviction about something" was in full bloom and on display. After the nominees had made their speeches, we were sent out of the room to wait for the outcome of the vote. When we returned, the Class Manager announced I had been voted Class President. My classmates exploded into cheers. Several Managers ran out of the room. I don't doubt they went looking for Class President historical information to see if a black man had ever been elected to the prestigious position. It was believed, at the time, I was either the first black or the second in the history of IBM to be chosen Sales Training Class President. The Michigan State grad told me I had won by a landslide. Mom's "humility seed" had paid off. When I returned to Birmingham, my Sales Manager had already heard about how well I had done on the presentation he nixed, and my election as Class President. I'm sure he credited himself for both of my accomplishments. The only credit he was due, in my opinion, was in motivating me to prove to him how wrong he was about black people. Shortly after my return, our Branch Manager assigned me to work for the Branch's first Hispanic Sales Manager.

After Cynthia had graduated from UAB with a degree in Mass Communications, she accepted a job offer from the largest radio station in Montgomery. Following, I asked for and received an opportunity to interview with IBM Montgomery's Branch Manager. During my interview, he told me he graduated from Auburn and was the Student Government Association President one year. He reviewed my resume, and we spent about 5 minutes interviewing. The rest of the time, at least thirty minutes, was spent talking about Auburn and my basketball experience. I got the job, to say the least.

During my eleven-year career with IBM, I managed multi-million dollar sales territories and was responsible for selling the company's portfolio of Hardware, Software, Wide Area Networking (WAN), Communications, and Local Area Networking (LAN) solutions. I sold directly to Information Technology (IT) Upper Level (i.e. C-Level) Managers, Middle Managers and End Users in the Government and Commercial sectors (Fortune 1000 companies). My ability to successfully address my clients' needs resulted in me receiving **14** IBM Branch and Regional Manager sales awards. I averaged **130%** over my annual quota during my tenure, became one of the company's first Professional Services (i.e. outsourcing) Sales Consultants, closed a **$1,000,000** database outsourcing contract with the State of Alabama, and a **$500,000** database migration outsourcing contract with an international apparel company. I also represented IBM on a thirty-minute special broadcast by WSFA TV entitled "Blacks in Corporate America." My television appearance was so well received, IBM flew in a Vice President to personally congratulate and thank me for representing the company so well.

Every five years, IBM held Family Dinners around the country for employees and their spouses. Cynthia was such a hit, at hers and my first IBM Family Dinner in Montgomery, with a company Vice President, some of my coworkers teased me and told me I was about to get promoted. When we got home, Cynthia shared she now understood why I loved working for IBM so much and spent so many long hours trying to do an excellent job for the company. She had become as sold on IBM as me. It turned out, my peers at the Family Dinner were correct about Cynthia's impact on the Vice President. Sure enough, I was promoted about a month later. Back then, when in a corporate setting, a spouse could either make or break their partner's career, in my view. Cynthia enhanced mine with IBM.

Right around my last year or so at Big Blue, I sold a computer system to the Governor's Office of the State of Alabama. Former Presidential nominee George Corley Wallace was serving his third and last term as Governor of the state. I had finished a meeting with Al Childs, the Governor's Chief of Staff when I realized I was about to be late for another appointment. Mr. Childs recommended I take the underground tunnel, which was a "restricted" passageway under the State Capitol. As I was walking through the tunnel, I could see mounted cameras shifting with my every move. Out of nowhere, the Governor and his State Trooper bodyguard, who was wheeling him down the hall, appeared. Suddenly, the Trooper drew his gun and said, "Halt! What are doing down here?" I told him I had received permission from Al Childs to use the corridor. The trooper got on his radio to confirm I had been approved to use the tunnel. (For all I know, I may have been the first non-government official to receive clearance to use the facility). Once my approval was confirmed, I had the opportunity to meet Governor Wallace. History rushed through my mind. This was the man who once said, "Segregation now,

Segregation tomorrow and Segregation forever." The same man whose "Stand in the Schoolhouse Door" speech, at the University of Alabama, decried the entrance of blacks entering the school, and desegregation in general. After introducing myself, there I stood shaking his hand. Governor Wallace said to me, "You're our IBM sales rep, aren't you?" I responded, "Yes, I am." The Governor told me I was doing a great job and to keep up the good work.

Alabama State Capitol Tunnel

Later, I sat down with Mom and told her about my chance encounter with Governor Wallace. I thought Mom would have something negative to say about him. To the contrary, she said, "Butch, don't let that man fool you. He's one of the shrewdest and smartest politicians I have ever seen. If you'll notice, he has changed political stance in the past, if it helped him get votes. He is a master at getting people riled up and emotional. People overlook how good of a politician he is." I was sitting there marinating on what I had just heard. It made a lot of sense, though, and nearly 30 years later, I saw Donald Trump execute

George Corley Wallace-like political strategy to, from out of nowhere, be nominated President of the United States.

As with anything in life, one cannot be successful were it not for the help of others. Many people at IBM aided my business and sales development and helped me close sales. The one individual that stood out was Joe Reese, a Senior Account Manager, who later became my Sales Manager. Blessed with a photographic memory, he remains the best salesperson I've ever come across. I assisted Joe once in a meeting involving an outsourcing deal with a Fortune 1000 apparel manufacturer. Towards the end of the session, the customer agreed to buy roughly $1.5 million in new IBM equipment. Joe told the Senior Executive we were presenting to, IBM had a new printer he wanted to show him. The Exec told Joe how much he loved his current IBM 3262 printers and there was no way he was going to replace them. Joe persisted, and unenthusiastically, the customer agreed to take a look at the new printer. The night before, Joe, James Semsey, who was the best IBM Systems Engineer I had been around, and I were in the office until about 10 P.M. preparing for the meeting. We ran tests on the new printer and did supply cost analysis. We learned, two of the new printers delivered greater throughput than one IBM 3262, and annual supply costs were dramatically lower. With this sales ammo, Joe had me share our findings with the Senior Executive. Next, Joe went for the close. The Senior Exec looked over the results and decided to buy two of the new printers. I was flabbergasted! Joe had taken a customer from a firm "No!" to a committed "Yes!" From that day forward, Rick

Sewell, an Account Manager and friend of mine, and I started referring to Joe as, "Yoda" from Star Wars fame. When Joe would walk by, we'd say, "Hail Yoda! The wise, powerful and omnipotent one."

My 10th year at IBM, tragedy struck Cynthia and me. Complications had arisen a month before our second child Gabrielle was to be born. Sadly, we lost her and Cynthia nearly died as well. During our misfortune, I had never seen as much courage and strong faith in God as Cynthia exhibited. We were humbled by the subsequent outpouring of love from family, friends and my IBM colleagues.

My 11th year at Big Blue, the company went in the red, financially, for the first time in the Corporation's history. The organization was in a state of flux, and morale was low. Headhunters were swooping in from all over the place to take advantage of the situation. I saw some of our most admired and valuable Salespeople and Managers leave the company. After being contacted by a headhunter, I anguished for a week or so, as to whether or not I should stay with IBM or leave the company. Cynthia found me crying in the laundry room one day as I struggled with my "stay" or "leave" decision. I decided to leave Big Blue and join General Electric (GE) and its Diagnostic Imaging organization. My sales office was in St. Louis, Missouri. By this time, God had blessed Cynthia and me with our third child, Dominique, named from the French meaning, "Of the Lord."

GE

When I hired on with GE in 1992, the company ranked fifth on the Fortune 500 list, right behind IBM. Revenues were $60.2 billion, and profits stood at $2.6 billion. From a revenue performance standpoint, the companies were eerily similar that year. Shortly after I moved to St. Louis, to begin my Diagnostic Imaging Sales Training, GE provided two house hunting trips, I had negotiated, to the city for Cynthia. I was living in an extended stay facility until the family arrived. On her second visit, Cynthia and I closed on a home in Chesterfield, a suburb of St. Louis. A few days after she had flown back to Montgomery, to pack and coordinate things with the moving company, I accidentally locked myself out of the house and left my cell phone inside. I remembered our real estate agent had shown us how the front windows of the house could be pushed outward to clean them from the inside of the house. I figured she might have left one of the windows unlocked. Fortunately, she had. I climbed up onto the ledge of the window, and as I was half way in the house, I heard someone yell, "Stop! Get down from there! I've called the police." I came back out of the window and informed the person, who turned out to be our next door neighbor, I was the new homeowner and had locked myself out. Seeing he was unconvinced, I told him that once I got inside the house, I would come back out with my closing paperwork to allay his concerns. He watched with a doubtful look on his face as I climbed into the house. I grabbed the paperwork from the closing, went back outside, and showed it to him. He called the police department to let them know the owner had locked himself out of the house. We had a good laugh about what happened. Truth be told, we were the only black family in the neighborhood, and I'm sure my neighbor stereotypically, thought, "One of **them** is trying to break into the house in broad daylight."

My Diagnostic Imaging training lasted six months. I spent about equal time in St. Louis and in Waukesha, Wisconsin where GE's Diagnostic Imaging manufacturing and related training facility were housed. I performed so well in the training program, the Senior Executive of the division, who was a former IBM'er, received Board approval to award me stock options. Receipt of stock options, which are typically reserved for Senior Management, was unprecedented for a GE "New Hire." The Senior Exec also placed me in the company's "Fast Track" Management Development program. He believed I had the potential to become GE's first or second Black Vice President, at the time. Things were going well at GE and on the home front. Cynthia and I were rapidly getting acclimated to the St. Louis area, and I picked back up being an Assistant Coach on Derek's (my oldest son) Little League baseball team.

Our second year in the city, St. Louis experienced the "Flood of the Century," had a 12-inch snowstorm, and an earthquake measuring around 4.3 on the Richter Scale. Those events combined with: being 600 miles away from our nearest relatives, Mom getting older and living alone, and me working about 70 hours a week, began to weigh on me. I was desirous of maintaining a healthy work/lifestyle balance and being closer to immediate family. I also found myself constantly comparing GE to IBM. It was like I had been married to IBM and had gone through a challenging divorce, then married GE and was comparing my new partner to the old. I would catch myself thinking, "We would never have done this at IBM." My mindset was not fair to GE. I decided something had to give. I shared my feelings with Cynthia and told her I felt it would be best for the family to move closer to Alabama. When I informed my bosses I wanted to get back to the Southeast, they searched for sales openings, but none were available. I took some time off to contemplate my next steps.

While I was off, I weighed staying in Corporate America against breaking out and doing my own thing (i.e. entrepreneurship). Heretofore, I'd been hesitant about starting my own business. Reason being, I had four mouths to feed and was doing well financially. If my business venture didn't pan out, I faced putting my family in a precarious financial position. When you roll the dice on entrepreneurship, you can't think like that. So, I decided on a middle of the road approach, which was Franchise ownership. I realized I had made millions of dollars for my employers and had received, by my calculations, roughly 2-3% commissions on my sales. I began to wonder how much I could bring in annually if I were my own boss. I researched Franchises I felt offered reasonable startup costs and yielded a stable rate of Return on Investment (ROI). Regarding

Corporate America, I was confident I could get on with the likes of AT&T, who was getting into the computer industry and was looking for talented sales people with strong IT backgrounds if need be. I knew I fit their bill, and my former Ma Bell experience would be a plus for them.

Of the Franchise opportunities I researched, I felt most comfortable with the start-up costs associated with Mail Boxes Etc. (now the UPS Store). After having successfully met the franchisor's initial financial requirements, the company sent a VP to St. Louis to discuss potential Franchise opportunities and financial details with me further.

The doorbell rang and the Mail Boxes Etc. Representative asked to speak with Eric Simmons. I replied, "Speaking." He was startled. Surely, a black man didn't submit the financials he had reviewed. He couldn't possibly own the multi-level home with landscaping originally done by the St. Louis Botanical Gardens, smack dab in the sprawling community of Chesterfield, Missouri where the median income was about \$80,000 in 1993[2] that he was visiting. I chuckled inwardly and offered him some water to put his mind at ease. Upon review of my net assets, instead of being offered one Franchise opportunity, I was offered two. One was in Chesterfield, and the other was to be in a yet to be built mall in Lithonia, Georgia. We agreed I would tour the Chesterfield store

---

[2] \$83,802 in 2000 per City-data.com

which was for sale. During our visit, I could understand why the store was only generating about $43,000 annually. It was in a strip mall in a stable area of Chesterfield, but the front of the facility did not face the main street entering the strip mall. Instead, the entrance was perpendicular to the main thoroughfare thereby making it difficult to see the location upon entry to the mini mall. After I had returned home, I called Aunt Regina to find out about the progress of the anticipated mall in Lithonia. I learned the project had been put on hold. After considering the circumstances of both stores, I opted not to proceed further with pursuing the Mail Boxes Etc. opportunities.

I decided to go ahead and start an aggressive job search in Atlanta. I submitted my resume to AT&T, and as I had figured, I heard back from the company almost immediately. A Human Resources representative called me to schedule an interview. On my way to Atlanta for the interview, I stopped by our old house to check in on Mom. Cynthia had been kind enough to let me move her there shortly after we moved to St. Louis. Following my interview with AT&T, I was offered a sales position, and I accepted.

AT&T

It felt great being back in the South. Atlanta was booming, and Cynthia and I were much closer to family now. About a month into my new job at AT&T, I received a phone call from Cassandra Hayes, a writer for Black Enterprise magazine, of which I was a subscriber. I had no idea how Ms. Hayes had gotten my number. She wanted to interview me for an article on how black executives were handling business entertainment with their customers when companies were increasingly cutting costs on such activities and slashing payroll. After receiving clearance from AT&T's public relations office to do the interview, I scheduled a date and time with Ms. Hayes for the discussion. Following, I was quoted in the magazine's November 1994 edition in an article entitled, "The new deal on business entertaining." An excerpt from the article reads, "AT&T's Simmons says that he has a personal litmus test – what he calls "the media test" – for all of his corporate conduct. What this means he says is "if my conduct was scrutinized, could I [later] support what I did?" This was another Mom "seed," and it summed up what my business approach was during my 30+ years in Corporate America.

Several months into my new job, I sensed something was wrong. I was primarily selling voice products, and although my department would mention AT&T's new data offerings, I didn't find myself selling any of them. About my fourth month on the job, I met with my Sales Manager and asked him when we were going to start aggressively selling the company's data products. He shared that was not the focus of the department I was in. Confused, I explained to him my primary reason for joining AT&T was so that I could sell data products. It was at that point, my Manager informed me there had been two organizations within AT&T that vied for my services. One was the Voice Department, which I was in, and the other was the Data Department. The Voice Department won out. We continued our conversation and realizing I had not been told about the scenario, my Manager gave me the contact information for the head of the Data sales group in Atlanta and gave me the opportunity to arrange for an interview.

I tried at least four times to reach the C-Level Executive responsible for the Data team to no avail. On perhaps my fifth attempt, I was able to land an interview. The Executive was a dynamic, well spoken, forward thinking black female. Shortly after my interview began, her phone rang. It was her husband on the other line. She told him she was interviewing an Auburn graduate who had been at the school around the same time as he. When the Exec said my name to her husband, he told her he had never heard of me. The Exec peeked at my resume and told her husband I had played basketball for Auburn. Again, he told her he had never heard of me. Curious as to who her husband was, I asked the C-Level for his name. She gave it to me, and I said, "You're married to "Fly" from Auburn? You've got to be kidding me. I know him." I said, "Tell him you're interviewing Flea and I said hello." She passed the information on, then looked at me and said, "My husband wants to talk to you." When I got the phone, I said, "Fly, this is Flea man. It's been a long time. How've you been doing?" I glanced up and saw Fly's wife shaking her head and mumbling, "Fly, Flea, Flea Fly; this is crazy." I continued to catch up with Fly and suddenly realized I was in the middle of a job interview.

I politely excused myself and resumed my conversation with his wife. It turned out; I had precisely the skills and qualifications she was seeking. I was offered and accepted a position within her organization which was responsible for Data Communications and Internet services.

About a week into my new job, I received a call from our mortgage lender about the new house Cynthia, and I was buying. He said, "Eric, there's something wrong with your debt to equity ratio. Don't worry about it, though, these things happen all the time." How could I not worry about my credit? I contacted the major credit bureaus and requested my credit reports. To my astonishment, there were over 30 purchases listed I had not made. Someone had stolen my identity. Having my identity stolen turned out to be a personal nightmare! When I explained my situation to my C-Level, she let me spend all workday, every day for a week on the phone trying to get my credit straightened out. The dollar amount of which I had been defrauded was large enough for me to get the Secret Service involved. I called the Secret Service for assistance, and to my amazement, someone picked up the phone! I remember thinking to myself, "If they are so secret, why the hell did they just answer the phone?" The Service was so heavily bombarded with identity theft matters they suggested I contact the local police in the city in which most of the debt had occurred. In my case, it was Dallas, Texas. I received tremendous help and support from the police officer I spoke with and managed to get the debt down to a point where Cynthia, the kids and

I could move into our new home a day or so before Christmas. It took me almost a year to completely clear up my credit and my name. Afterward, over a three-year period, I, periodically, would receive phone calls looking for the person who had used my name and my social security number.

I advanced steadily through the fledgling Data organization and saw it triple in size to about 100 people. During my time in the group, I sold AT&T's first Virtual Private Network (VPN) and developed an online sales training manual and supporting video to teach our company's 2,000 salespeople how to sell the company's Data and Internet offerings. I rolled out the video nationally around the time our second son (Kevin) was born. Just when things couldn't get any better, it seemed, AT&T announced it would be "right-sizing," a fancy term, in my mind, for letting people go. Company employees who had over 20 years of service, as I recall, were offered a "buyout" package. Unsure about what other steps might be forthcoming, I began an aggressive external job search.

I landed a Sales Manager job with a business unit of Blue Cross and Blue Shield of Georgia, selling a data solution for physician's offices. My old IBM buddy Rick Sewell was my hiring Manager. The "seed" here was, "Treat people like you would want to be treated because you might need them one day." One year into the job, Blue Cross sold the business unit to a company in Florida that wanted all of its employees to be based at its headquarters location. Not looking to move to Florida, I decided I was going to try to find a job that would enable me to fulfill a long-desired business goal of mine which was to travel internationally.

MCI

At this stage in my Corporate career, I could not believe I was in the process of looking for another job. I was certain when I joined IBM; I would be a "lifer" with the company. I felt, if I were ever to leave Big Blue, I would probably work for no more than one or two companies during my career. Corporate America, as I once knew it, was changing dramatically all around. Loyalty between company and employee was impacted by things such as globalization, downsizing, corporate greed, and profit being more important than employee retention to name a few. Those employees who were fortunate enough, especially in high-tech fields, had options and so "job hopping" became more prevalent. Job hopping was no longer frowned upon as much, by hiring companies, but often was viewed as an indicator of added skills a new employee was bringing to the table.

As I searched online for my next job, I came across a job description that floored me to such an extent; I had to share it with Cynthia. It was as if someone had taken my business resume and posted it on the Internet. The position was for a Senior Sales Consultant position with MCI, the second largest telecommunications company in America. Within a week after submitting my resume, I received a call from MCI's HR Department which wanted to schedule a telephone interview between me and Ralph Johnson, MCI's Sales Director in its Global Solutions Sales organization. When I had my interview with Ralph, during introductions, he shared when he first saw my resume; he thought I had plagiarized the job description. After our meeting, Ralph acknowledged my skills and qualifications were commensurate with what he sought. He arranged for me to fly to MCI's Headquarters in Ashburn, Virginia to meet and interview with his Senior Level Manager.

When I arrived at Dulles Airport, Ralph was there to greet me. He was every bit as impressive in person as he was over the phone. It was apparent from the onset; he was knowledgeable and polished in the areas of Data Communications Sales Management and International Business. Upon meeting the Senior Executive, I found her to be equally impressive. The three of us hit it off right away, and I believe it was due to each of us having extensive Data Processing/Communications experience. At one point during the interview, I drew on a flip chart my vision of how the Global Solutions Sales organization could sell its VPN offering to MCI's customers and teach its internal sales force about the solution. Thoroughly impressed with my presentation, Ralph looked at his boss and said, "I told you, didn't I?" to which she replied, "You're right Ralph. He's everything you said he was and more." The Exec offered me a job on the spot, and I gladly accepted.

Not long after I started my new job, I met my nine Senior Sales Consultant counterparts at a team meeting at Headquarters. While I was impressed with my peers' backgrounds, they were blown away with mine. Each of us reported to Ralph and carried a $15 million annual sales quota. Our primary responsibility was to understand our clients' needs and subsequently delivery to them global networking solutions to address their requirements. We were to call on C-Level Executives and above, at Fortune 1000 companies.

I had been on the job a few months when on a team call, Ralph shared one of the Senior Sales Consultants had closed a $1 million deal. After the call, Ralph called me and said, "Eric, I just realized everyone on the team has been working an International opportunity and traveling abroad, and I haven't sent you anywhere yet. I'm going to assign the next international opportunity that comes across my desk to you."

My First International Business Trip

Early one morning, Ralph called to tell me he had an opportunity he wanted me to work on involving a Division of Shell Oil in Brussels, Belgium, the "Capital of Art Nouveau." He needed me to gain a thorough understanding of the customer's requirements, then develop a "Capabilities Overview" to present to the client in Brussels. A few weeks later, I flew to Brussels to make my presentation. Ralph had concluded some business in Germany and flew in to join me for the customer session, as did Reba Mudavadi, a Technical Support team member from Headquarters. My presentation to Senior Level Data Communications Managers of the Division went so well; we closed $1,000,000 in business with the customer. Ralph had previously suggested I stay in Brussels for a few days after the meeting to tour the city. That night, as several fellow employees and I, were headed to dinner, the driver of the car I was in lost track of our peers we were following, and we ended up in front of the United States Embassy in Brussels. I got out of the car and videoed the front of the building then realized it might not be a good idea to do so. Once we had our dinner location figured out, my peers and I heartily celebrated our sales victory. To this day, I don't recall the ride back to my hotel.

One evening, Reba and I had gone walking looking for a place to have dinner when all of a sudden, a heavy downpour ensued. We scurried onto the steps of a restaurant with an overhang to protect ourselves from the rain. We looked inside and decided to eat at the establishment. I went downstairs to the restroom, which I had no idea was unisex, and a woman walked out of a stall. Thinking I was in the ladies room, I turned to leave, and a man came out of another stall. Imagine the surprised look on my face! After washing my hand in the communal fountain, as I was leaving, outside a lady was handing out hand towels. I gave her a tip with some loose francs I had in my pocket. As I turned to walk away, the woman grabbed me by the arm and thanked me profusely for my tip. Wondering if I had grossly over compensated her, I started converting francs to dollars, in my head, to determine how much I had given her. Out of nowhere, the woman told me I was handsome and looked just like the man she had fallen madly in love with, years ago. Then, she began telling me more about her lover. Initially, I was paying only half attention, but as she got deeper into her story, she took me on a magical ride with her through World War II. As I looked into her eyes, and upon her face, worn by age and what must've been a very hard life, I could envision how beautiful she was when she was young. She told me she had met a dashing young black U.S. Army soldier and the two fell madly in love. Excitedly, they made plans to marry and ultimately flew to the United States to tell his family the good news. The soldier, who was from Kansas, introduced his beautiful European girlfriend to his parents. Sadly, she was rejected by them because of her race and returned home all alone. Reverse racism, go figure. The lady's story was so heartbreaking, upon my return to the dinner table, I was visibly shaken. Reba asked me what the matter was. When I retold the woman's story, my coworker felt it was as beautiful and sad as I had. I shared with Reba; the woman seemed as though she were referring to my Dad who had served the Army in Germany, was from Kansas and whom I resemble. Reba convinced me it was just an amazing coincidence.

As we were finishing up our dinner, the elderly lady and her daughter stopped by Reba's and my table on their way out. The mother said to Reba, "You have a very kind and handsome husband." Reba told her we weren't married, and that we were coworkers. After the ladies had left, Reba said, "Eric you're right! You did bring back memories to that woman. She's still very much in love with that soldier she told you about." I remarked, "I know." When I returned to the United States, I shared the story with Dad. He didn't say one word. Years later, when I would try to see if he indeed had been the soldier, he would never say a thing.

There were areas of Belgium that were so clean; you probably could've eaten off the streets. Also, the architecture of the buildings was breathtaking! My stay in Brussels and time to tour the city got cut short, however. Ralph called me in a panic to tell me he needed me to go to Paris immediately to assist MCI's sales team on an opportunity that was going down the tubes. I informed him I'd get on a flight right away. Well-versed in International travel, Ralph told me, in the interest of time; it would be quicker for me to take the bullet train to Paris, which I did.

PARIS, FRANCE

Hurtling along at 300 km/h the bullet train I was on was moving so fast, I couldn't video the gorgeous landscape. I was amazed at how smooth the ride was. When I arrived in Paris, I could not believe the long waits in lines or queues as Parisians refer to them. I hailed a taxi and gave the driver the address to the hotel MCI's Paris sales team had arranged for me. Navigating recklessly through traffic, before I knew it, the driver was going right through the Louvre. I remember thinking, "This is where some of the greatest art in the world is located, including the Mona Lisa, and this guy is driving like a bat out of Hades right through the courtyard of the facility. How can this be?" During the drive, I was awestruck as I looked left, right, front and behind me at the sites of the beautiful "City of Lights." I saw a tall building to my left that was brownish in color. I asked the driver if it was the Eiffel Tower and he said it was. I had always thought it was a silver structure. Without warning, the driver suddenly made a U-turn and headed right towards the Eiffel Tower. When he stopped, at the hotel I was staying at, we were right across from the plaza of the Tower!

When I handed the driver some Belgium francs to pay him, he told me he could not accept them; they had to be French francs. I thought a franc was a franc. At the time, Europe was undergoing changing its currency to the Euro, and I don't know if that was the reason why the driver would not accept the Belgian francs or not. No problem I thought. I went inside the hotel to take out a cash advance on my company credit card and then do a currency exchange. To my surprise, I was informed I had overextended the credit on my card. I had gone over my limit during my current trip. I called MCI's travel agency and had them increase the limit on my card. When I went out to pay the taxi driver in French francs, he gave me this look like, "Dumb a#$ American."

That night, when I called Ralph to let him know I was in Paris, I shared my story about the driver and the francs. I got a good chewing out for not having turned in my business expenses before I left to travel to Europe. During the call, Ralph told me the reason why he wanted me in Paris was to assist the local Account Team with explaining Global Solutions' capabilities to Senior Management at Air Liquide, a global gasses, and technology company. The sales opportunity was at risk because the customer did not understand our Virtual Private Network's self-healing capability (i.e. the ability of a network to reroute traffic to other available circuitry in a span of milliseconds when a circuit is cut). The next morning, I received an update from the Account Team. I spent the rest of the day and part of the evening in my hotel room putting together a customized presentation around the customer's stated requirements. I was using my planning and preparation "seed." At dinner, I reviewed my presentation with the Account Manager and Technical Support Engineer. Afterward, I went back to the hotel, called the family and got an update on Derek's Little League Baseball practice and Dominique.

The next morning, when we arrived at Air Liquide's Headquarters, my peers and I signed in at the front desk. For some reason, it was taking an inordinate amount of time for my "Guest" pass to be processed. I later learned Air Liquide was waiting on information from Interpol regarding my background. The Account Team made me aware Air Liquide had been a recent victim of a terrorist attack at one of its plants and was taking extra security measures at Headquarters. As I walked through the revolving door to head to the meeting room, the door stopped. I thought there had been some mechanical problem. When I walked out, I asked my colleagues if they knew what had happened. They informed me I had just walked through a bulletproof door and had been body scanned for weapons. After having been checked by Interpol and body scanned in a bulletproof revolving door, I was sure I was in a James Bond movie.

After Air Liquide's Senior Manager over the project had arrived, everyone around the table began introducing themselves. When my turn came, I said, "Bonjour, Monsieur Dubois." Immediately, Monsieur Dubois started addressing me in French. He went on and on, and when he stopped, I said, "With all due respect Monsieur Dubois, that's all the French I've got." The entire room burst into laughter. Monsieur Dubois replied, "My apology Eric. You spoke it so well; I thought you were French." I stated, "No need for an apology. I do have one request, though. May we continue the meeting in English?" More laughter throughout the room. After having made a good first impression on Air Liquide's Senior Manager, my presentation went extremely well, and MCI was awarded a $500,000 contract. Before my return to the U.S., the MCI Account Manager I had been working with, took me on a four-hour tour of the city. We went to Napoleon's tomb, the shopping district, walked side streets and drove places tourists probably don't get to see. He also explained to me the history behind some of the architecture in the city.

HONG KONG

The most challenging, and fun, sales opportunity I have ever worked on was a strategic Managed Network project for FedEx Asia. The company's objective was to have a sole service provider completely manage its data network in Hong Kong and Singapore. Per the terms of the customer's Request for Proposal (RFP), the winning company would be responsible for roughly 200 pieces of equipment and provide 99.95% network reliability and redundancy. Our primary competitors for the business were Singtel and Hong Kong Tel, both of which were Asia-Pac companies with significant presence in the region. Equant was also competing for the project. I was Sales Lead for MCI and was responsible for coordinating all internal sales meetings domestically and internationally.

During our first call with the customer, the scope of the project was presented. FedEx Asia's Senior Manager responsible for the project told us, on the call, he was concerned about dealing with a U.S. based company and preferred dealing with an entity that was either Headquartered in the Asia-Pacific region or had a significant presence there. My takeaway was, "MCI you don't have a snowball's chance of getting our business." My competitive juices were flowing!

Following our call with the Senior Manager and his team, I established weekly calls with my team. When we needed clarification from the customer about something, I would arrange for a call with them commensurate with their time zone and schedules. This meant, due to the 13-hour time zone difference between the customer and most members of my team, I would have to start the call typically between 3:00 and 4:00 A.M. Eastern Standard Time. Not much of a coffee drinker, I would load up on orange juice with crushed ice to stay awake. Over time, as a result of me and my team's due diligence regarding the project, the Senior Manager began to warm up to our U.S. based company.

About five months into the sales cycle, on one of my team calls, our Technical Team lead suggested we propose our Standard Managed Network Services solution in the company's RFP response. I strongly felt otherwise and pushed back hard during the call, and recommended a "Custom Solution." In other words, we were going to build a "customer specific" network. This was my "stand your ground seed when you have a conviction about something." Things got contentious to the point, between the Technical Lead and I, Ralph had to intervene. My rationale was, I had noticed on several of our calls with the customer, the Senior Manager hinted at envisioning a one-of-a-kind network like no other. During my team call, it was agreed I would convene a call with the client to validate their desire. Sure enough, the customer confirmed what my sales "ears" were hearing. Following the call with the Senior Manager and his Team, our Technical Lead apologized to me for doubting my assessment of the customer's vision. I told him, "Don't worry about it. That's why they pay you and me the "big bucks" – so that we can sort things out to come up with a solution to delight our customers." Later, the Technical Team came back to me with a bang up network design I felt confident I could sell and which would win the business.

Around May 2, 2000, we submitted MCI's response to FedEx Asia's RFP. About a month later, the company contacted the RFP respondents to announce a meeting in Hong Kong for each organization to present their proposed networks. I made my arrangements to fly to Hong Kong. In the ensuing weeks, I put together a PowerPoint "Qualifications Overview" presentation, researched Chinese culture and proper Asian business conduct, in preparation for the upcoming meeting. Instinctively, I was utilizing the "always be prepared and even over prepare seed" implanted in me by Mom.

On the day of my departure, and several hours before I left my home, I received a call from MCI's Account Manager for FedEx Asia. He informed me he felt he could present MCI's solution during the RFP response meeting. The Account Manager, who had perhaps been on only two calls during the six-month long response development, would have been massacred in the meeting. There was no way in the world he could articulate the intricate design of the network we had put together for the customer. Combine that with the amount of work I had put into the RFP response and my extensive knowledge about what we were recommending; there was no way I was turning back now. I told the Account Manager, I am coming to Hong Kong!" and hung up on him.

My flight to "Fragrant Harbor," as Hong Kong is referred, was fantastic. The service from the flight attendants on Singapore Airlines was like nothing I had experienced before in air travel. The 14-hour trip left enough time for me to watch the movie, "The Green Mile" twice. I also took advantage of the exquisite food and free-flowing champagne. As I videoed the plane's landing in Hong Kong, I thought for a minute we were going crash into the water, not realizing Hong Kong International Airport's runway extended into Kowloon Bay. On the way to my hotel, I watched from a distance as large cargo containers were being effortlessly moved about on cranes. From my vantage point, they looked like small Lego blocks being moved around on a large table. When I arrived at the Hong Kong Ritz-Carlton, the staff treated me as if I were royalty. After getting some rest. I prepared for my upcoming sales presentation.

The next morning at MCI's Hong Kong sales office, I met the local Account Team and Managing Director. We had a preplanning meeting to review the company's proposed solution and to outline the order of speakers. The Account Manager thanked me for coming to Hong Kong and informed me he would be doing the presentation. I was thinking, "Over my dead body!" I gave a mini-presentation of what I was going to say, and after I had finished, the Managing Director said, "Eric that was incredible!" He then looked at his Account Manager and sternly said, "Eric's giving the customer presentation."

When we arrived at FedEx Asia's headquarters, at least two of our competitors had already given their presentations. There were about 15 people in total from the customer's and MCI's team at the session. When the time came to present, MCI's Managing Director led off. I was next in order on the agenda, and I gave my "Qualifications Overview" PowerPoint presentation. When I finished, FedEx Asia's Senior Manager looked at his Management team, pointed at me, and said, "You see this guy? You see this guy right here? He's the reason why we should consider doing business with MCI!" The reporting Managers had been given their marching orders in no uncertain terms, it seemed to me. At the end of our meeting, the Managing Director invited FedEx Asia's Senior Manager to lunch. The Exec told us he would join the MCI team in about thirty minutes.

As the MCI contingent walked over to a nearby hotel for lunch, the Managing Director lauded me for my presentation and told the MCI'ers he felt confident we would be awarded the business. Although Hong Kong had been under British rule for 99 years, and English was a commonly spoken language, all of the items on the menu at the hotel were in Chinese. The Managing Director, whom I learned over lunch I had replaced after he was promoted to Hong Kong, assisted me with ordering my meal. He recommended, at a minimum, I try drunken prongs. I sat fascinated as the chef prepared what looked to me like shrimp on steroids. The meal was the best I'd had in a business setting. Over lunch, FedEx Asia's Senior Manager complimented me on my presentation and informed us we had won the business – barring any significant issues, particularly legal, during contract negotiations. He agreed to sign a Memorandum of Understanding (MOU) to that effect. Toward the end of lunch, I offered the Senior Manager a tour of MCI's Network Operations Center (NOC) in Cary, North Carolina. He told me, if he were in the United States (at FedEx's Memphis Headquarters) in the foreseeable future, he would take me up on my offer.

I spent seven days in Hong Kong and had a chance to see some of its most interesting sites. I fell in love with the view from Victoria Peak overlooking the city and Hong Kong Harbor. The hustle and bustle of the business district of Hong Kong reminded me a lot of Manhattan. The Managing Director suggested I go over to the mainland to see Big Buddha, one of the largest statues in China. I recalled an American student had been cane whipped, a few years back, in public by Chinese authorities in nearby Singapore, so I said to myself, "There is no way on Earth this black man is going over to the mainland alone!" Therefore, I declined the Director's suggestion. Overall, the people in Hong Kong were incredibly friendly, and the Ritz made my stay quite pleasant. I must admit, I did have trouble eating with chopsticks, especially peanuts, but those around me never seemed to mind and would invariably hand me silverware. I enjoyed my time in Hong Kong so much so, I plan to take Cynthia there one day.

Following my return to the States, I gave Ralph an in-depth debrief about my business trip. We strategized about next steps, to cement the deal, and agreed I would continue trying to convince the customer to visit the Cary NOC, which we both felt was a must. About a month later, I received a call from the Senior Manager informing me he was going to be at FedEx's Headquarters for a few days, and schedule permitting, he would try to visit our NOC. Ultimately, the Manager's schedule opened, and I arranged for a tour.

Ralph joined me for the meeting at the Cary NOC, which I had not been to before. I was given a tour of the facility and was blown away. I had been in NOCs before, during my tenure at AT&T, but this one was the most impressive I had seen. There were monitors all over the place tuned in on CNN to keep abreast of weather patterns and news. The place was so quiet you could hear a pin drop. Part of my tour, before the customer arrived, involved seeing the room where communications were managed for the Federal Aviation Administration (FAA), whose contract MCI had at the time. It was impressive watching the monitoring of air traffic all around the world.

When FedEx Asia's Senior Manager arrived, Ralph and I prepped him on what he would be seeing. During the tour, I could tell the Director was pleased with the solution he was planning to buy. Towards the very end of his visit, the Exec said, "Eric, show me this self-healing capability you've been telling me so much about. I'd like to see it in action." I did some asking around to see if there were any network outages I could show the Manager and sure enough a large cable outage had just happened on the east coast. I walked the customer over to a Technician's desk, and we watched the network instantaneously begin "self-healing" by rerouting and load balancing itself to accommodate the part of the circuitry that had been cut. It was mind blowing to see. The Senior Manager told us we had sealed the deal and that he would let both company's lawyers proceed with finalizing the contract. We had just won **$25,000,000** in business!

Things did not turn out to be all roses, however. Not long after my sale, it was learned MCI's CEO and CFO were part of an accounting and investor fraud scandal. This discovery sent the company into chaos. Ultimately, our Global Solutions sales group was dismantled.

Chapter 19

Mom Becomes Ill

After Dad had retired, he moved to Detroit to be with Grandma Nannie Belle whose health was failing. Shortly after she passed away, he called and told me he sought to get back to the South and wanted to see if he could stay at our house in Montgomery with Mom. Not sure how Mom would feel about such, I called to get her thoughts. She had no objections. I ran things by Cynthia to get her opinion, and she didn't mind either. One day, I received a call from Dad. He told me an ambulance was at the house to take Mom to the hospital, and he was going to follow them. He shared he would give me a call as soon as he got to the hospital. About an hour later, he called to tell me Mom was being transported to UAB's Medical Center. I knew something extremely severe was going on because UAB's facility was one of the tops in the country. I left work driving like a bat out of hell to UAB.

Dad followed the ambulance from Montgomery to Birmingham, so, I met him at UAB. When I got there, he told me the attending Physician believed Mom had suffered a brain aneurysm but wouldn't know for sure until tests were done. Several hours had passed before the Doctor gave us an update. Mom had indeed suffered a brain aneurysm. Dad and I feared the worst. The Doctor told us Mom might not be able to speak and/or she might suffer paralysis following surgery. My heart sank. Worried about whether he had locked the front door of the house when he left in such a hurry, I told Dad that next morning he could drive back to Montgomery, and I would stay at the hospital with Mom.

Mom's Doctor provided me with another update and assured me Mom would live. He told me he had never lost a patient. When he left, I remember thinking, "Here goes another Doctor so full of himself, he thinks he's God." A nurse who overheard the Doctor's and my conversation walked up to me and said, "He's right. He's never lost a patient. He's one of the most renowned Neurosurgeons in the world. In fact, people come from around the world to UAB to have him operate on them. He's performed surgery on Kings and Princes. Your mother is in good hands with him." After the surgery, the Doctor made me aware the operation was a huge success. He informed me instead of one brain aneurysm; Mom had suffered two and was fortunate to be alive. The Doctor told me, during the procedure, he was determined he wasn't going to lose my Mom. I could tell he was very proud his record of having never lost a patient, remained intact.

Mom's stay and follow-up rehab at the hospital were anticipated to be about one month. Overflowing with patients in critical care status, the hospital arranged for me to stay in an apartment up the street, which was a renovated hotel. I didn't realize the facility was set up for family members whose loved ones were waiting for procedures such as kidney or heart transplants and/or were predicted to die. I heard a lot of incredible stories in the laundry room, and I became close to several people during my stay. More times than not, when I would see people in the lobby or parking lot leaving it was because their loved one had passed away. I gained a better sense of, and appreciation for, how delicate and precious life truly is. After a month of rehabilitation, Mom was cleared for me to take her back to Montgomery. Her Doctor felt it best she was in an environment she was comfortable in and knew. Dad had gone back to Detroit to be with Aunt Norma who was very ill herself.

Mom had become incapacitated and barely knew who I was. Her role and mine had completely reversed. I had become the parent, and now she was the child. Now, I was feeding her, changing her diapers, wiping the drool from her mouth, giving her medicine, and baths. Words can't begin to describe how sad and painfully excruciating it was for me to see my Mother, such a vibrant and intelligent woman, be in such a helpless state. I cried rivers of tears and prayed incessantly. Mom had at least 12 different medications which I had to be extremely diligent about her taking. It concerned me immensely the amount of medicine she was receiving.

Her Physical and Speech Therapists put together a program to help Mom regain somewhat of a normal life. I had to teach her; her ABCs, how to speak, how to count, how to write and how to walk all over again. Cynthia and the kids would drive down from Atlanta, when they were out of school, on weekends to help me out. Weeks went by, and Mom made slow but steady improvement. About six months into her rehab, one day I told Mom it was time for her shower. After I had gotten her settled in, I reached for a towel and turned towards Mom. She looked at me and said, "Young man. How dare you. Can't you see I'm a lady, and I'm taking a shower?" I said, "Yes Ma'am. My apology." I ran up the hall jumping up and down yelling, "She's back, she's back. Mom's back." Immediately, I called Cynthia to give her the great news. Mom's faculties were coming back. Rarely, had I ever been so happy. The next few months, Mom's progression was nothing short of a miracle. Seeing how far she had come from the time of her surgery to the point of where she was now, reassured me there was a God.

Mom fully recovered and was sharp as she was before her aneurysms. She suffered no loss of speech, didn't have a lisp nor partial paralysis. She went on to live another strong seven years before she passed away.

Chapter 20

Closing

While I had a good run in Corporate America and had accomplished much, I was ready to walk away. So, at the age of 58, I started my own company, Eric Simmons Enterprises, Inc. The goal of which is to provide assistance to prospective high school athletes in packaging their marketing information to increase their exposure to college coaches. I was giving back to sports, which had provided me so much. The company got off to a good start, but Dad became ill, and I ended up spending nine months in Montgomery with him until he passed away at the age of 90. Perhaps I'll try to "kick start" my company again or just relax and enjoy my free time with my wife, kids, and grandchildren.

So, there you have it Derek, Dominique, and Kevin. That's your Pops story. I must share, I am proud of each of you and your accomplishments to date. Derek, I fervently believe you will be the youngest black Head Baseball Coach in Division I in the next few years. It wouldn't surprise me if a Major League Baseball (MLB) team were to pick you up either. Dominique, I look forward to calling you, Dr. Dominique Simmons when you complete Physical Therapy school. Kevin, I hope you follow your dream and apply to Medical School next year, and become Dr. Kevin Simmons.

I have no doubt your ancestors in heaven, especially Grammy, are smiling with the knowledge the "seed" of their lives is flowing through each of you and that you're, "Not Far From The Tree."

References

- Fortune Magazine 1981 and 1992 "Fortune 500" list

- Fortune Magazine – "How IBM Teaches Techies to Sell"

- NCAA – "Probability of Competing Beyond High School"

    o   http://www.ncaa.org/about/resources/research/mens-basketball

- Chesterfield, Missouri Median Income

    o   http://www.infoplease.com/us/census/data/missouri/chesterfield/

    o   Source: 2011-2015 American Community Survey 5-Year Estimates

    o   http://www.city-data.com/city/Chesterfield-Missouri.html

- USBE magazine.   "MS. SIMMONS' CHILDREN" By Sylvester Foley III

- Black Enterprise magazine.   "The new deal on business entertaining" November 1994 page 74 and The Free Library: https://www.thefreelibrary.com/The+new+deal+on+business+entertaining%3B+integrity,+results+and+costs...-a015891534

- Thom Gossom Jr. Biography

    o   http://www.imdb.com/name/nm0331699/bio

- Wikipedia and Wikiwand

CPSIA information can be obtained
at www.ICGtesting.com
Printed in the USA
FSHW022318070119
54876FS

9 780692 953303